The Best of Vegan Cooking

Other Books by Priscilla Feral:

Dining With Friends: The Art of North American Vegan Cuisine (2005; co-authored with Lee Hall).

Published in the United States by
Friends of Animals
Nectar Bat Press
Darien, Connecticut

Cover photograph by Jane Seymour

This book is dedicated to you.

Thank you for welcoming *The Best of Vegan Cooking* into your kitchen, and for accompanying us on our adventure of choosing, preparing, and sharing the vegan dishes in these pages.

D1301010

Acknowledgements

My heartfelt thanks to:

Lee Hall, whose friendship, amazing writing, editing and ideas made the book possible.

Donna Thigpen, who worked so hard to organize this book and attend to so many details, and whose advice has been invaluable.

Jane Seymour, my daughter, whose beautiful photographs appear throughout this book. Jane, who has a wheat allergy yet appreciates fine vegan food, prompted me to take a special interest in risotto recipes.

Bob Orabona, whose enthusiasm for food and cooking helped spirit the book to be published.

Linda Long, who did so much to contribute recipes from great chefs, bringing sensational talent to the book—along with Linda's outstanding photographs.

Trish Sebben-Krupka, whose culinary talents inspired me, and whose skills as a chef produced eight extraordinary recipes for this book.

Dustin Garrett Rhodes and Nancy Rice, who worked diligently on testing some recipes, developing others, and putting them all together; and Paul Saccone, who contributed key outreach efforts.

Finally, thanks to Mark Zuckerman for designing the book and seeing it through production.

Contents

Main Dishes   19

Pasta   39

Risotto 47

Vegetables and Side Dishes 55

Pancakes, Breads and Muffins 67

Desserts 79

Ice Cream and Sorbet   91

Glossary   97

Introduction

*T*his book celebrates the work of a number of chefs and authors who are developing vegan cuisine into a fine art. As you'll soon see, it's an art you can learn and share, even if you've never yet considered yourself a chef.

With an emphasis on daring combinations of fresh fruits and vegetables and a vibrant spectrum of grains, the keynote to *The Best of Vegan Cooking* is variety. You'll be drawing on global influences, creating new variations on Italian classics. Like the invigorating Asparagus and Spring Pea Risotto. And who could possibly come across Chef Trish Sebben-Krupka's Carmelized Leek and Shiitake Risotto without wanting to gather friends together?

Delight in the surprisingly smooth combination of Watermelon and Tomato Salad. Then, let Chef Jesús González regale your kitchen with a recipe for Authentic Mexican Tortillas, accompanied by suggestions for classic toppings, followed by a little something to cool the palate: Berry Parfait with Avocado Cream.

Make a summer day more memorable with our irresistible Blueberry-Pomegranate Sorbet. Or bring a rich, traditional aroma into your kitchen with Chocolate Marbled Pound Cake.

A collaborative effort is a special joy, and this book has many. Susan Wu, co-founder of greater Philadelphia's SuTao Café, loved the festive Spiced Pumpkin Cheesecake in Friends of Animals' debut cookbook, *Dining With Friends: The Art of North American Vegan Cuisine,* and came up with the variation introduced here as Two-Layer Thanksgiving Cheesecake by using half the amount of creamy pumpkin filling recommended in our earlier recipe, then adding a new top layer. The result, as you'll see, is beautiful. Claudette Vaughan, an Australian activist and editor of the *Abolitionist Online,* has offered Coconut Cake—for which we provide the icing.

Linda Long, author of *Great Chefs Cook Vegan,* searched everywhere for Mignardises—the most wonderful of vegan dessert truffles, derived from natural ingredients including vanilla beans and raw cashew butter—and found them, courtesy of Chefs Charlie Trotter and Matthias Merges. Baby Artichokes Provençal Style appear courtesy of *New York Times* food columnist Mark Bittman, author of *How to Cook Everything Vegetarian.*

Chef Mary Lawrence, the owner of the personal chef service Well on Wheels, brings us Mediterranean Pasta with Garlic Greens and Butter Beans, as well as Irish Mashed Potatoes with Greens and a new chapter in the venerable history of Irish Stew. Mike Behrend, chef for the very first vegetarian restaurant in San Antonio and greatly appreciated by the staff members of our primate sanctuary, offers us the most tempting Sweet Potato Gnocchi.

These are just a few of the recipes here in *The Best of Vegan Cooking,* all designed to be healthful for your body, uplifting to your soul, lovely on your table, and delicious to your taste buds. One of the aspects that will make your art especially beautiful is that it's also a declaration of peace to all conscious beings.

Which brings us to what "vegan" means. Donald Watson and a few good friends coined the term in 1944. They joined the first and last letters of the word "vegetarian" because veganism starts with vegetarianism and carries it through to its logical conclusion: living and preparing food without any need for animal products, and seeking, as far as possible, harmony with the planet and all its inhabitants, whether two-legged, four-legged, winged, finned, or feathered. Watson was a great idealist who said if the commitment to "non-exploitation" would take hold, it would be the greatest peaceful revolution ever known.

It couldn't come a moment too soon.

For in these times, disruptions to peace on Earth go beyond what we've conventionally thought. There's the cutting down of trees, the loss of clear waters, and the dangers to Earth's unique web of beings: bees who pollinate the almonds, birds who bring seeds across the miles. What we decide to eat plays an essential role in keeping the birds on the wing and the bees abuzz.

More and more, people are coming to understand the relationship of animals to the environment, and that we don't truly control, but merely take part in, that relationship. And that's why traditions in so many social settings are changing. People now know animal farming causes a substantial portion of greenhouse gas, in addition to the harm done to the hapless beings in whom it trades. We are gaining a full appreciation of the world's water and natural space, so much of which is diverted to feed crops, thus creating conflicts which can only be addressed by changing the way we sustain ourselves.

Now, the focus is on life-affirming foods, fresh, whole, and lively, picture-perfect as they are nutritious. Now, it's about our gratitude for knowing our meal really matters. Now, we're eating as though the Earth and the animals who live on it count.

If we all ate and celebrated mindfully—learning to produce wonderful food directly from grains and the thousands of other plants that grace our planet— we could greatly reduce energy use, and make our world a far more joyful spot in the universe. We could each spare about an acre of trees per year, too. And trees absorb extra carbon dioxide and provide homes for animals.

Many people who change their diets make learning about nutrition yet another benefit. The core principle for good health is to eat a wide variety of vegetables and fruits, which, according to experts in nutrition and diet, can provide all the vital vitamins and minerals needed by people of all ages.[1]

We hope and expect the people you meet, know, and hold dear will enjoy the dishes featured in these pages. Make the most of the recipes by seeking, if you can, fresh seasonal produce at farmers' markets or from your personal or community gardens. You can find organic tofu, free from genetic modification, in most groceries, co-ops, and Asian food shops—just right for Marinated Tofu and Pineapple Kabobs or Spicy Barbecued Tofu Triangles. Soy milks and creamers, like vegan margarine, are also becoming ubiquitous. Vegan cream cheese (such as "Better Than Cream Cheese") is somewhat less common, but a call to your local natural food shop should help you locate it.

May *The Best of Vegan Cooking* show just how well your commitment to peace blends with opportunities to prepare healthful, delicious, attractive dishes you'll want to prepare and share again and again.

Priscilla Feral

President
Friends of Animals

1 For a comprehensive guide to vegan nutrition, see Brenda Davis, RD and Vesanto Melina, MS, RD, *Becoming Vegan: The Complete Guide to Adopting A Healthy Plant-Based Diet* (2004), in which foremost vegetarian dietitians present up-to-date findings on protection against cancer and heart disease, the body's fat and protein requirements, meeting calcium needs without dairy products, what vegans need to know about vitamin B12, balanced vegan diets for infants, children, parents, and seniors. Also helpful, especially from the standpoint of data references, is *Plant Based Nutrition and Health*, written by Dr. Stephen Walsh (2003), research scientist and long-time nutritional consultant to The Vegan Society.

Soups

Manhattan Vegetable Chowder

Photograph: Linda Long

Manhattan Vegetable Chowder

Serves 6 to 8

❖ ❖ ❖ ❖ ❖ ❖ ❖ ❖ ❖ ❖ ❖ ❖

3 tablespoons olive oil

1½ cups diced onion

½ teaspoon smoked paprika

1 cup diced carrot

1 cup diced celery

1 cup fennel, cored, halved and thickly sliced

1 cup diced zucchini (courgettes)

1 teaspoon fresh thyme

½ cup dry white wine

6 cups light vegetable stock

2 pounds fresh plum tomatoes, peeled, seeded and diced, with juice (or one 28-ounce can diced tomatoes)

1 bay leaf

½ teaspoon dried marjoram

½ teaspoon dried oregano

Pinch of dried chili flakes

2 cups peeled, diced russet potato

1 teaspoon finely grated orange zest

1 tablespoon fresh orange juice

Hot pepper sauce, to taste

This refreshing, satisfying and slightly spicy soup, by Trish Sebben-Krupka, evokes Manhattan Clam Chowder. Bacon and clams are replaced with chunky fresh vegetables, tomatoes, fresh herbs and spices, and a hint of sweet orange. This soup freezes well, and tastes even better the next day.

Preparation:
Heat olive oil in a large saucepan over medium heat. Add onions, smoked paprika and a pinch of salt, and cook, stirring occasionally, until soft (but not browned), about 10 minutes. Add carrots, celery, fennel, zucchini and thyme, season with a little more salt, and cook for about another 5 minutes, stirring often. Pour in white wine, increase heat to high, and bring to a boil. Add vegetable stock, tomatoes, bay leaf, marjoram, oregano and chili flakes. Return to a boil, add potatoes, and reduce heat to medium. Simmer for 30 minutes, add orange zest and juice along with a dash of hot pepper sauce, and continue to simmer until vegetables are soft.

Remove from the heat and add parsley. Taste and adjust seasonings with lemon juice, salt and freshly ground pepper. Serve with crackers.

¼ cup chopped fresh parsley

A squeeze of fresh lemon juice

Salt and freshly ground pepper,
to taste

Miso Tempeh Nori Soup

Serves 4 to 6

❖ ❖ ❖ ❖ ❖ ❖ ❖ ❖ ❖ ❖ ❖ ❖

2 tablespoons white miso paste

½ cup Nori (thin, dried, edible seaweed sheets), cut into strips

1 tablespoon lemon juice

1½ cups Shiitake mushrooms, cut in strips

½ cup green onions, chopped

2 cups baby spinach

6 cups vegetable broth

1 tablespoon peanut or untoasted sesame oil

2 tablespoons tamari

1 cup tempeh, cut in cubes

1½ teaspoons grated ginger

There's nothing like an exceptionally good miso soup; this one was adapted from a recipe by Gonzalo Mendoza at Rancho La Puerta Fitness Resort. Bits of Shiitake and tempeh give this delicious soup bite.

Preparation:
Sauté the tempeh and mushrooms in oil until the mushrooms are soft. Add the vegetable broth with the miso, nori and ginger.

Bring to a boil, reduce heat and simmer for 5 minutes. Add the spinach, green onion, tamari and lemon juice. Stir a few seconds, season to taste with salt and pepper and serve.

Black-Eyed Pea & Winter Greens Soup

Serves 6

❖ ❖ ❖ ❖ ❖ ❖ ❖ ❖ ❖ ❖ ❖ ❖

8 ounces black-eyed peas

Bouquet Garni (1 bay leaf, 3 sprigs fresh thyme, ½ teaspoon whole peppercorns in cheesecloth pouch, tied with twine)

2 quarts light vegetable stock

3 tablespoons extra virgin olive oil, divided

2 cups leeks, thinly sliced, white and light green parts only

1 cup carrots, peeled, halved lengthwise and sliced

1 cup celery, halved lengthwise and sliced

1 cup roasted, peeled and chopped red, orange or yellow bell pepper

3 cloves garlic, peeled, finely chopped, divided

½ teaspoon each: chili powder, smoked paprika, marjoram leaves, oregano, Cajun seasoning

¼ cup dry white wine

2 cups peeled, diced tomatoes (use fresh if in season or canned tomatoes drained)

1 tablespoon hot sauce, or to taste

4 cups greens, a mix of collards, chard, beet greens, well washed and thinly sliced 1-inch lengths

Another delightful recipe by Trish Sebben-Krupka. This soup tastes best when it has rested overnight in your refrigerator. The recipe doubles or triples easily to serve a crowd, and freezes wonderfully.

Preparation:

Soak black-eyed peas in fresh, cold water to cover for 8 hours; or use the quick-soak method, bringing beans and water to cover to a boil, cooking 10 minutes, removing from heat and soaking for 1 hour. Drain and rinse beans.

Place beans in a large stockpot with bouquet garni and vegetable stock. Bring to a simmer; cook for 45 minutes or until beans are almost tender. Salt lightly after 30 minutes.

Meanwhile, heat 1½ tablespoons olive oil in a medium sauté pan. Add leeks, carrots, celery, peppers and 2 cloves garlic. Cook for 5 minutes over medium heat. Add spices; cook an additional 5 minutes. Season with a little salt and pepper. Deglaze pan (release juices that have browned on the bottom) with white wine and set aside.

When beans are nearly cooked, add vegetable mixture, tomatoes and hot sauce to stock pot, along with enough water to cover bean and vegetable mixture. Season with a little salt. Continue to simmer as you prepare the greens.

Wipe sauté pan clean, and heat remaining 1½ tablespoons olive oil. Add remaining clove of garlic, and sauté lightly for about 1 minute—do not allow garlic to brown! Add greens all at once with another pinch of salt, and cook over medium-high heat until greens are softened and release liquid. Using tongs, remove greens and add to soup. Discard liquid in pan.

Simmer soup for an additional 15 minutes or until all ingredients are cooked through. Add lemon juice and parsley. Taste and adjust seasonings as necessary—salt, pepper, hot sauce, or a little more lemon juice.

2 tablespoons fresh lemon juice

¼ cup fresh parsley, finely chopped

Salt and freshly ground pepper to taste

Cauliflower and Potato-Leek Soup

Serves 4

❖ ❖ ❖ ❖ ❖ ❖ ❖ ❖ ❖ ❖ ❖

1 tablespoon vegetable oil

1 medium onion, chopped

1 pound leeks (white and pale green parts), well rinsed and chopped

2 medium russet potatoes, peeled, cut into ½-inch dice

½ head chopped cauliflower florets

4+ cups vegetable broth

2 teaspoons grated fresh ginger

Salt to taste

1 teaspoon fresh lemon juice

4 thin lemon slices, seeded

1 tablespoon very thinly sliced green onion tops

This creamy soup surprises with hints of ginger and lemon. Amazing all by itself or serve with some fresh-baked bread (see our Whole Wheat Baguette recipe).

Preparation:
In a large pot, heat oil over medium heat. Add onion and cook over low heat, stirring occasionally, until golden brown, about 20 minutes. Add leeks, potatoes, cauliflower and 3 cups broth and ginger. Bring to boil. Cover, reduce heat and simmer until potatoes are tender, about 20 minutes. Remove from heat; let mixture cool slightly, about 10 minutes.

Using slotted spoon, transfer all solids in saucepan to food processor. Process until very smooth, stopping to scrape down side of work bowl as necessary. With machine running, gradually add liquid in pan to processor. Return soup to saucepan. Bring to simmer, adding remaining broth for desired consistency. Season with salt and stir in lemon juice. Ladle into bowls. Garnish each with lemon slices and green onions if desired.

Corn and Potato Chowder

Serves 4 to 6

❖ ❖ ❖ ❖ ❖ ❖ ❖ ❖ ❖ ❖ ❖ ❖

2 tablespoons corn oil

2 leeks, finely chopped

2 tablespoons flour

2 ½ cups vegetable broth

½ pound unpeeled boiling potatoes, cut into ½-inch cubes

2 stalks of celery, finely chopped

3 ears corn, kernels cut off the cob, or 1 ½ cups frozen corn, thawed

1 cup soy milk

1 cup soy creamer

1 teaspoon celery seeds

1 teaspoon sea salt

Fresh ground black pepper to taste

This chowder, rustic yet smooth, is both deliciously satisfying and easy to prepare.

Preparation:

Heat corn oil in skillet and add chopped leeks. Cook 1 minute or more until soft. Turn down heat and stir in flour until combined. Remove from heat and set aside.

Put the vegetable broth, potatoes and celery in a large pot. Add chopped leeks mixture. Bring to a simmer over medium heat, cover, and cook about 10 minutes, stirring occasionally.

Add the corn, soy milk, soy creamer, celery seeds, salt and pepper. Return to a simmer, and cook about 5 to 8 minutes more, stirring occasionally. Serve immediately.

Aunt Trish's Pasta e Fagioli

Serves 6

❖ ❖ ❖ ❖ ❖ ❖ ❖ ❖ ❖ ❖ ❖ ❖

2 or 3 tablespoons olive oil

1 cup finely chopped onion

1 cup finely chopped celery

A big pinch of salt

3 or 4 cloves of garlic, finely chopped

A nice big pinch of red pepper flakes

1 large can plum tomatoes, preferably San Marzano, lightly crushed by hand

4 cups of light vegetable stock

2 cups water

2 or 3 cans of small white beans, or Mina's favorite, Roman beans

A splash of white wine, optional

1 cup of elbow macaroni

A big pinch each of dried oregano, dried marjoram

½ cup chopped fresh parsley

A handful of torn fresh basil, if available

Salt and freshly ground pepper

Here's an excellent opener to a memorable meal, courtesy of Chef Trish Sebben-Krupka. There are as many types of pasta e fagioli as there are cooks who make it, so feel free to adjust this dish to your liking. Sometimes we like it a little spicy; sometimes soupy, and sometimes very thick. Letting it rest about ten minutes before you serve it will help the flavors develop. In Italy, *pasta e fagioli* is traditionally served during the summer months, at room temperature.

Preparation:
Heat olive oil in heavy-bottomed stockpot over medium heat. Add onions, celery and salt immediately so the vegetables sweat out some of their liquid. Sauté for about 8 minutes, reducing heat if necessary to prevent browning. As celery and onions are becoming soft, add garlic and crushed red pepper. Turn the heat to medium-high, and sauté for one more minute. Add tomatoes that you have poured out into a bowl and lightly smashed with your hands. Alternatively, you can add the tomatoes whole and mash with your potato masher or a fork. Add broth, water and dried herbs; simmer over medium-low heat for about 30 minutes.

Turn heat to high; add beans and pasta, and wine if you are using it. Cook for 10 to 15 minutes, or until pasta is just cooked. Immediately remove from heat. Add parsley, and basil if you have it. Season to taste with salt and pepper. Allow to rest for 10 minutes before serving.

To serve, ladle into a bowl and drizzle with a bit of olive oil. Grind on a little more pepper and garnish with toasted bread crumbs.

Butternut Squash Soup

Serves 8

❖ ❖ ❖ ❖ ❖ ❖ ❖ ❖ ❖ ❖ ❖

3 tablespoons olive oil

3 medium carrots, peeled and diced

2 stalks celery, diced

1 medium yellow onion, diced

3 large garlic cloves, minced

2 pounds butternut squash, peeled, seeded and cut into half-inch cubes

One 28-ounce can whole peeled tomatoes

2 cups cooked cannellini beans (one 15-ounce can)

8 cups light-colored vegetable stock

1 small head Savoy cabbage, core removed and leaves thinly shredded (8 cups)

1 bunch Swiss chard, stems removed and discarded, and leaves coarsely chopped (6 cups)

1 bay leaf

Salt and freshly ground pepper to taste

Grated vegan parmesan for serving

This soup is the ultimate cold-weather comfort food. With greens and beans, it also happens to be a nutritious, one-pot meal. Serve with crusty bread.

Preparation:
In a large pot, warm the olive oil over medium heat. Add the carrots, celery and onions, and salt the vegetables lightly. Cook, stirring occasionally, until the vegetables are slightly softened and the onion is translucent, about 5 to 7 minutes. Add the garlic and cook until fragrant, about 1 minute. Add the butternut squash, tomatoes, cannellini beans, broth, cabbage, chard, and bay leaf. Stir to combine the ingredients.

Bring to a boil, cover and cook over medium heat for approximately 45 minutes, or until all the vegetables are tender.

Remove bay leaf.

Using a stick blender, purée the soup to desired consistency. Season with salt and pepper to taste. Serve with grated vegan parmesan.

Salads

**Himalayan
Red Rice Salad
With Cranberries**
Photograph: Linda Long

Himalayan Red Rice Salad With Cranberries

Serves 4

❖ ❖ ❖ ❖ ❖ ❖ ❖ ❖ ❖

Water or vegetable broth for cooking rice

3 bay leaves

½ cup red rice, rinsed and drained

1 teaspoon olive oil

2 tablespoons minced fresh ginger

½ cup celery, finely diced

1 tablespoon minced garlic

½ cup chopped green onion

½ cup carrots, finely diced

½ cup red bell pepper, finely diced

¼ cup dried cranberries

2 tablespoons toasted nuts (chopped pine nuts, almonds or walnuts)

1 tablespoon balsamic vinegar

1 tablespoon tamari

This recipe combines many flavors and textures to create a delightful, light and surprising rice salad. Perfect all by itself or served as a side dish. This recipe was adapted from a recipe created by Chef Jesús González at Rancho La Puerta Fitness Resort.

Preparation:

Follow instructions on red rice package—with the addition of the bay leaves. Due to the various types of red rice available, cooking times will vary between 25 and 45 minutes—although any type of red rice is suitable for this recipe.

Bring water or broth to a boil, along with bay leaves. Sprinkle in the red rice. Bring to a boil again. Turn down heat and cover pot, simmering without stirring until grains are tender and water is absorbed. Remove bay leaves.

To toast nuts, pre-heat oven to 400 degrees F. Spread nuts in a single layer on a baking pan (preferably one with walls). Heat for several minutes or until the nuts start to turn golden. Shake the pan halfway through toasting.

In a sauté pan over medium heat, cook the garlic and ginger in oil about 5 minutes, until lightly browned. Combine raw vegetables with rice, toasted nuts, cranberries, vinegar and tamari in a bowl. Mix well. Allow to sit for about 15 minutes. Serve.

Broccoli Rice Salad With Almonds and Sesame-Ginger Dressing

Serves 6 to 8

❖ ❖ ❖ ❖ ❖ ❖ ❖ ❖ ❖ ❖ ❖ ❖

1 cup uncooked brown rice (wild rice works well too)

1 pound broccoli florets, cut small

½ cup chopped red bell pepper

¼ cup sliced or slivered almonds

⅓ cup rice vinegar

2 tablespoons soy sauce

1 tablespoon sesame oil

2 tablespoons water

2 teaspoons fresh ginger, minced

2 cloves garlic, minced

⅛ teaspoon red pepper flakes (or to taste)

With highlights of ginger and sesame, this salad makes a tangy and healthful side dish or an easy lunch.

Preparation:
Cook the rice according to package instructions. Set aside to cool.

Steam or blanch broccoli until just tender, about 5 minutes. Let cool. Then add the broccoli, chopped red pepper and almonds to the cooled rice.

Combine the remaining ingredients in a small mixing bowl. Pour over the rice mixture and toss to combine. Refrigerate until completely chilled.

May be served alone or over a bed of fresh salad greens.

Bulgur Wheat Salad

Serves 4

❖ ❖ ❖ ❖ ❖ ❖ ❖ ❖ ❖ ❖ ❖

1 cup bulgur wheat

2 small raw red peppers, minced

1 medium yellow onion, chopped small and sautéed in a small amount of extra virgin olive oil about 5 minutes

1 bunch scallions, chopped small

¼ cup fresh lemon juice

2 tablespoons Cortas Pomegranate Molasses (pomegranate paste)

3 tablespoons extra virgin olive oil

Chopped parsley and Herbamare (herb seasoning salt) to taste

If you haven't yet had an excuse to try pomegranate molasses, here it is. (You can use it to pour over vegan ice cream as well.) This slightly sweet grain salad is adapted from a recipe created by Maggie Vosgueritchian from The Organic Market in Westport, Connecticut.

Preparation:

Pour 1½ cups of boiling water over 1 cup of dry bulgur wheat. Add ½ teaspoon salt, cover and set aside for 30 minutes.

Add prepared bulgur wheat, red pepper, onion, and scallions in a bowl. Then add lemon juice, pomegranate paste, olive oil and herb seasoning. Sprinkle with a little chopped parsley.

Grilled Corn and Black-Eyed Pea Salad

Serves 4

❖ ❖ ❖ ❖ ❖ ❖ ❖ ❖ ❖ ❖ ❖ ❖ ❖

3 ears fresh corn, shucked, silk removed

2 cups cooked black-eyed peas (canned are fine)

1 red bell pepper, finely diced

1 yellow bell pepper, finely diced

½ red onion, finely diced

¼ cup chopped fresh Italian parsley

1 tablespoon finely chopped cilantro

Zest and juice of 1 lemon

A dash or two of your favorite hot pepper sauce

Extra virgin olive oil, to taste

Salt and freshly ground pepper, to taste

Thanks to Trish Sebben-Krupka for this versatile salad recipe. This summer salad makes a wonderful light lunch when served over well-chilled greens with a drizzle of extra virgin olive oil. It also makes a fine condiment for grilled veggie dogs.

Preparation:
Heat grill or grill pan to medium-high. Grill corn until lightly charred in places, turning frequently, about 5 minutes. (You may also roast in a 400 degrees F oven for about 10 minutes with equally good results.)

Set corn aside until cool to the touch. Remove kernels by standing cob on your cutting board on its stem end, and running a sharp knife down the sides of the cob at a 10 degree angle. This should leave you with whole kernels of corn.

Place corn kernels, black-eyed peas, red and yellow bell pepper, onion, parsley and cilantro in a medium mixing bowl. Add lemon zest (remove zest with a microplane grater, or peel yellow skin from lemon, being careful to leave the bitter white "pith" behind, and chop finely), lemon juice and a drizzle of olive oil. Taste, then season with salt, pepper, hot sauce and a little more olive oil if necessary.

Watermelon and Tomato Salad

Serves 4

❖ ❖ ❖ ❖ ❖ ❖ ❖ ❖ ❖ ❖ ❖

2 cups seedless watermelon, in 1-inch cubes

2 cups grape or cherry tomatoes, halved lengthwise

1 lemon, juice and zest

1 tablespoon extra virgin olive oil

Sea salt, small pinch

Freshly ground black pepper

½ cup thinly sliced (julienned) fresh mint leaves

For your next gathering, share a salad that's completely unexpected and delicious. The sweetness of watermelon enhances the tomatoes' sweetness.

Preparation:
Combine watermelon, tomatoes and salt in a chilled bowl.

Whisk lemon juice, zest, oil and pepper and drizzle over fruit. Sprinkle with mint, and toss gently. Do not refrigerate; serve within 30 minutes on chilled salad plates.

Watermelon and Tomato Salad

Photograph: Jane Seymour

Herbed Wild Rice Salad With Cherries, Pears and Apricots

Serves 6

❖ ❖ ❖ ❖ ❖ ❖ ❖ ❖ ❖ ❖

1 cup wild rice or combination wild and other rices, cooked and cooled

1 carrot, finely chopped

½ red onion, diced

1 cup snow peas, sliced in half

1 pear, sliced

⅔ cup dried or fresh cherries

4 apricots, sliced

⅓ cup Italian Herb Dressing (see the recipe that follows)

Salad greens (optional)

This rice salad blends together tangy, sweet and savory for an absolutely divine result.

Preparation:
Prepare rice according to instructions. Let cool completely.

Combine all ingredients and toss with rice. Let sit for at least 1 hour refrigerated. Serve over salad greens or alone.

Italian Herb Dressing

2 cloves garlic, minced

1 teaspoon dried tarragon

1 teaspoon dried marjoram

1 teaspoon dry mustard

½ teaspoon salt

¼ teaspoon pepper

½ cup olive oil

2 tablespoons red wine vinegar

Preparation:
Combine all ingredients in a jar with a tight lid. Shake the jar well. Alternately, whisk ingredients together well. Let stand for 1 hour at room temperature, then chill. Shake before serving.

Aioli Potato Salad

Serves 4 to 6

❖ ❖ ❖ ❖ ❖ ❖ ❖ ❖ ❖ ❖ ❖ ❖ ❖

2 pounds small red-skinned potatoes

1 cup chopped scallions

1 cup finely chopped celery

1 cup (or less) vegan mayonnaise

2 tablespoons fresh lemon juice

1 ½ tablespoons pressed garlic

1 teaspoon (or less) salt

1 teaspoon freshly ground black pepper

Optional: 1 tablespoon fresh, chopped chives

Aioli is the garlicky mayonnaise whose name is derived from the Provençal *alh*—garlic. Here, it is enhanced with celery, scallions and chives, and dresses up a small harvest of potatoes.

Preparation:
Cook potatoes in large pot of boiling salted water until just tender, about 20 minutes. Remove from heat, and while still warm, cut into quarters. Add scallions and celery and toss with potatoes.

Mix remaining ingredients in separate bowl, add to potato mixture and toss. Cover, and chill to allow flavors to blend.

Garnish, if desired, with fresh, chopped chives.

Sweet Potato Salad With Crystallized Ginger

Serves 4

❖ ❖ ❖ ❖ ❖ ❖ ❖ ❖ ❖ ❖ ❖ ❖

DRESSING

½ cup red wine vinegar

2 tablespoons light-flavored oil (grapeseed, walnut, soy or safflower)

1½ tablespoons agave nectar

2 teaspoons tamari

1 teaspoon grated fresh ginger

1 large pinch of ground red pepper

SALAD

1 pound sweet potatoes, peeled and cut into ¼-inch by ¼-inch pieces

½ cup scallions, thinly sliced

2 tablespoons crystallized ginger, finely julienned

The French Broad Food Co-Op in Asheville, North Carolina offered samples of this dish just before the holiday season; but just one bite and you'll want to enjoy it all year long.

Preparation:

For dressing, combine ingredients in a small bowl, mix well and let stand for at least 1 hour.

For salad, steam sweet potatoes over boiling water until tender, about 8 minutes. Plunge them into ice water to stop cooking, then blot dry with cloth.

In a medium-sized bowl, mix the sweet potatoes, scallions and crystallized ginger; add the dressing, toss and refrigerate for at least 1 hour before serving.

Main Dishes

Marinated Tofu and Pineapple Kabobs
Photograph: Linda Long

Marinated Tofu and Pineapple Kabobs

**Serves 3
(yields 6 to 7 kabobs)**

❖ ❖ ❖ ❖ ❖ ❖ ❖ ❖ ❖ ❖

1 pound extra-firm tofu, pressed and cut into 18 to 21 1-inch cubes

1 pineapple, cut into 1-inch cubes (enough for three pieces for each skewer)

1 large red pepper

1 large red onion

6 to 7 bamboo skewers (soak bamboo skewers in water for 30 minutes before using to prevent burning)

MARINADE
2 tablespoons extra virgin olive oil

1 small-medium shallot, chopped fine

1 clove garlic, minced

Grated zest from l lemon

1 lemon, juiced

1 teaspoon dried basil

⅓ teaspoon dried thyme

¼ cup vegetable broth

Sea salt and freshly ground black pepper

The added grilled pineapple makes this recipe especially delicious. Soaking bamboo skewers for 30 minutes prevents burning.

Pressing Tofu:
Tofu is pressed to extract water, create a firmer texture, and allow more absorption of marinade. Stand the block of tofu on its edge and slice horizontally into 2 equal slabs.

To press, place a clean towel on a baking sheet or cutting board. Place tofu sheets on the towel; cover with another towel. Gently press down on the towel to remove water. Remove damp towel and place two layers of fresh towels on top of tofu. Carefully place a bowl or other weight on top of the towels to press down on tofu. Let sit for at least 15 minutes.

Preparation:
In a baking pan, mix marinade ingredients. Place tofu cubes in the pan and coat all side with marinade. Cover and refrigerate several hours or overnight. Cut pepper and onion into 1-inch chunks, and steam vegetables for 1 to 2 minutes until just tender. A microwave works well for steaming.

Remove tofu from marinade, and thread 3 tofu chunks onto each skewer, alternating with pineapple chunks and vegetables.

To cook, place skewers on a flat grill sprayed with non-stick cooking oil. Brush lightly with oil and grill over medium heat for about 10 minutes, turning every couple of minutes to brown and cook on all sides. Leave kabobs on bamboo skewers and serve on a plate with cooked Jasmine rice.

Roman Beans and Rice

Serves 6

❖ ❖ ❖ ❖ ❖ ❖ ❖ ❖ ❖ ❖ ❖

1 pound of dry Roman beans

½ cup extra virgin olive oil

½ cup onion, chopped

½ cup green pepper

½ cup carrot, chopped

4 large cloves garlic, chopped

½ teaspoon dried oregano

½ teaspoon crushed chipotle chile pepper flakes

2 teaspoon sea salt

Ground black pepper

1 teaspoon tomato paste

15-ounces tomato sauce

1 cup hot water

Roman beans are also known as cranberry beans. They're nutritious and flavorful and they cook more quickly than many other dried beans.

Preparation:

Sort and wash beans. Add 6 to 8 cups of hot water. Boil 10 minutes, then turn off heat and set aside for 4 hours. Drain water from beans.

Heat oil in a large saucepan. Add onion, green pepper, and carrots and cook over medium heat, stirring vegetables until they begin to acquire a golden color, about 12 to 15 minutes. Add garlic, oregano, crushed chipotle chile pepper flakes and simmer a few minutes.

Stir in tomato paste and tomato sauce. Bring to a simmer. Season with salt and pepper and cook about 2 minutes. Stir in beans, add hot water and bring to a boil. Then reduce heat, cover and simmer, stirring beans and sauce occasionally until beans are tender, about 30 minutes or more.

Serve with hot cooked rice and corn bread.

Garam Masala With Chickpeas

Serves 4

❖ ❖ ❖ ❖ ❖ ❖ ❖ ❖ ❖ ❖ ❖

1 red bell pepper

1 yellow onion

2 tablespoons olive oil

1 tablespoon garam masala

1½ teaspoons curry powder

1 tablespoon Florida Crystals sugar

28-ounce can crushed tomatoes

One 15-ounce can chickpeas

2 teaspoons salt

Garam Masala means "hot or warm spice." Our gentle version of the classic Indian dish is at its best when served over basmati rice.

Preparation:
Over medium heat, sauté chopped pepper and onion until tender—about 5 minutes. Reduce heat to low, then add garam masala, curry powder and sugar; sauté for 2 more minutes, stirring constantly to combine spices. Add tomatoes and chickpeas, then return heat to medium-high—cooking until hot. Reduce heat to low and simmer for 15 minutes. Add salt and stir well.

Curried Tofu

Serves 4

❖ ❖ ❖ ❖ ❖ ❖ ❖ ❖ ❖ ❖ ❖ ❖

1 teaspoon brown mustard seed

Pinch fenugreek seed

1 pound tofu, extra-firm, cut into cubes

1 large yellow onion, ¼-inch dice

2 garlic cloves, minced

2 limes, zest and juice

2 tomatoes, large and ripe, ½-inch dice with juice

1 cauliflower head, cut into florets

½ pound white mushrooms, quartered

2 tablespoons curry powder

1 teaspoon turmeric powder

1 tablespoon canola or grapeseed oil

1 tablespoon ginger, grated

¼ bunch cilantro, chopped

One 8-ounce can coconut milk (use light, if desired)

Is there anything more versatile than tofu? Tofu can take on a variety of textures, depending on how it's prepared—and the flavor possibilities are infinite. Thanks to Chef Matt Murray of California for another intriguing recipe.

Preparation:

In a large skillet over medium-high heat, heat oil. Add mustard seed and fenugreek. Once the mustard seed begins to sputter, add onion, ginger and garlic. Sauté briefly, until onion becomes transparent.

Add curry powder, turmeric, mushrooms, tomatoes, lime juice and zest. Simmer several minutes, adding water if necessary.

Add cauliflower, tofu and coconut milk. Simmer 3 to 4 more minutes. Stir in fresh cilantro and serve.

Options: You can marinate tofu overnight in curry paste and grapeseed oil; or bake in a 375 degree F oven for 15 to 20 minutes, or fry quickly using same marinade before adding to dish.

Gobi Matar

Serves 4

❖ ❖ ❖ ❖ ❖ ❖ ❖ ❖ ❖ ❖ ❖

1 cauliflower, large head, cut into florets

1 red onion, small dice

2 ounces canola or grapeseed oil

1½ teaspoons curry powder

1½ teaspoons garam masala

1½ teaspoons fennel seed

Pinch crushed red pepper flakes

1 garlic clove, minced

1 teaspoon ginger, minced

½ lemon, zested

1 teaspoon black pepper, fresh cracked

½ cup green peas, blanched

¼ bunch cilantro leaves, chopped

"Gobi" means cauliflower and "matar" means peas. These two healthful and complimentary vegetables star in California Chef Matt Murray's mouth-watering recipe.

Preparation:
Pre-heat oven to 400 degrees F.

Mix oil, ginger, garlic, lemon zest and spices together in a large bowl.

Toss cauliflower and onions with spice mix to coat well. Spread out into roasting dish and place in oven. If using a convection oven, roast for about 15 minutes—otherwise, roast for about 25 minutes. Stir at least twice while roasting. Roast until cauliflower is tender but still firm.

Toss in peas and cilantro, stir to warm peas and serve. If necessary, return to oven for a brief minute to insure peas are warmed through.

Sweet Potato Gnocchi

Serves 4 to 6

❖ ❖ ❖ ❖ ❖ ❖ ❖ ❖ ❖ ❖ ❖

2 pounds sweet potatoes

About 11 ounces all-purpose flour

1 teaspoon nutmeg

1 tablespoon brown sugar

½ teaspoon cinnamon

2 tablespoons extra virgin olive oil

2 cloves of garlic minced

4 tablespoons fresh basil

1 teaspoon salt

1 teaspoon black pepper

½ teaspoon oregano

2 cups crushed canned tomatoes

"Green" is a mother-and-son restaurant located in San Antonio, Texas that opened in January 2006. In 2007, the restaurant was named Best New Restaurant by the *San Antonio Express-News* Critics' Choice Awards. This delicious, fragrant gnocchi, by Chef and co-owner Mike Behrend, will tell you why.

Preparation:

For gnocchi: Cut sweet potatoes in half and boil in salted water. Peel potatoes, mash and add nutmeg, brown sugar and cinnamon. Add flour and knead until dough is smooth (but don't overwork the dough). On a floured table, roll dough out to a thickness of ¼-inch. With a knife cut into 1-inch squares, and drop into boiling water. Remove the gnocchi with a strainer when they begin to float. Add sauce and serve.

For the sauce: Place a large sauté pan over medium heat. Add olive oil, then garlic, then tomatoes, then herbs. Bring to a simmer.

Grilled King Oyster Mushrooms

Serves 4 to 6

❖ ❖ ❖ ❖ ❖ ❖ ❖ ❖ ❖ ❖ ❖

GRILLED KING OYSTER MUSHROOMS

1½ pounds King Oyster mushrooms or portobello mushrooms

Fresh thyme sprigs

½ teaspoon minced Thai chile pepper

2 teaspoons salt

¼ cup olive oil

CHARRED JALAPEÑO OIL

1 tablespoon grilled jalapeños, seeded and stems removed

½ cup olive oil

⅛ teaspoon salt

AVOCADO

Juice of 3 limes

4 firm, ripe avocados, peeled and pitted

GARNISH

Salt to taste

Lime juice

8 to 10 fresh sprigs of thyme, stripped of leaves

Thanks to Chef Jean-Georges Vongerichten, who prefers the simplest, classic ingredients in "novel, even startling" combinations that are yet appealing to anyone who likes to sample new dishes. Here is a perfect example, from *Great Chefs Cook Vegan* by Linda Long. This dish is gorgeous and delightful, its ample yet finely sliced mushrooms complemented by the essence of zesty jalapeño and fresh, cool avocado slices.

Preparation:

To make the Grilled King Oysters: Place whole mushrooms in a glass casserole dish and top with a few thyme sprigs, chile, and salt. Drizzle oil over the top and cover with plastic wrap. Place dish in a warm place for 30 minutes. Heat a grill pan and grill mushrooms each side until tender. Remove from grill and cool for 15 minutes. Slice the mushrooms into thin strips.

To make the Charred Jalapeño Oil: Put jalapeños, oil, and salt in a blender. Purée until smooth and strain through a sieve to remove pulp; set aside.

To prepare the Avocado (four avocados): Lightly sprinkle lime juice over the avocados to keep them from oxidizing while preparing the plating.

How to plate: Warm oval or oblong serving plates. Thinly slice the avocados. On a piece of parchment paper that is slightly larger than the serving plate, alternate 8 mushroom slices and 7 avocado slices, beginning and ending with a mushroom slice. Note that other amounts can be used if desired. Invert onto the serving plate that has been warmed and further warm briefly in a 250-degree F oven for 2 minutes. Remove and brush liberally with the Charred Jalapeño Oil, sprinkle delicately with salt, drizzle with lime juice, and sprinkle thyme evenly over dish.

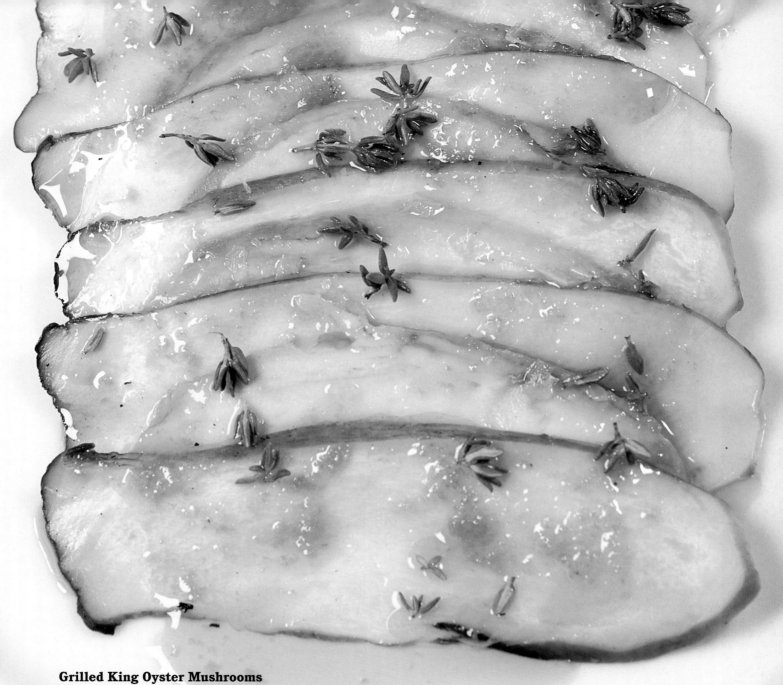

Grilled King Oyster Mushrooms

Photograph: Linda Long

Butternut Squash, White Bean and Kale Ragout

Serves 4 to 6

❖ ❖ ❖ ❖ ❖ ❖ ❖ ❖ ❖ ❖

1 large (3 pounds) butternut squash

2 tablespoons Earth Balance or other vegan margarine

2 tablespoons maple syrup

2 ½ teaspoons cider vinegar

1 teaspoon sea salt (or to taste)

1 teaspoon ground black pepper

Pinch of cayenne pepper (or to taste)

2 tablespoons extra virgin olive oil

4 large leeks (white and light green parts only)

4 large garlic cloves minced (or use a garlic press)

2 teaspoons rosemary (fresh or dried)

2 (15-ounce) cans cannellini beans, drained and rinsed

2 cups vegetable broth (or use vegan bouillon cubes and prepare according to instructions)

¾ pound kale, chopped (approximately 6 cups)

⅓ cup dried cranberries chopped (plus additional berries for garnish)

Adapted from *New York Times* recipe, this stew is hearty, healthful, and simply wonderful. A meal in itself.

Preparation:

Pre-heat oven to 425 degrees F. Dissolve vegan bouillon in hot water according to package instructions. Peel squash, then halve squash and scoop out seeds. Cut flesh into 1-inch cubes.

Spread cubes out on a large, rimmed baking sheet. In small saucepan, combine vegan margarine, syrup, 1 teaspoon vinegar, salt, ½ teaspoon black pepper and cayenne. Cook, stirring, over medium-high heat until margarine; pour mixture over squash and toss to coat evenly. Roast, tossing occasionally, until squash is very tender and caramelized at edges, about 30 minutes. In a large skillet, warm olive oil over medium heat. Add leeks, garlic, rosemary and a generous pinch of salt. Cook, stirring occasionally, until leeks are very soft and not at all browned, about 15 minutes. Add beans and broth and simmer for 10 minutes. Stir in kale. Simmer until kale is cooked down and very tender, about 10 to 15 minutes. Stir in squash and chopped cranberries; season with remaining 1½ teaspoons vinegar and ½ teaspoon black pepper. Garnish with additional cranberries and a small pinch of sea salt. Serve.

Vegetable Carousel Torte With Pommes Soufflés Filled With Peas

Serves 4 (depending on molds used)

❖ ❖ ❖ ❖ ❖ ❖ ❖ ❖ ❖ ❖ ❖

VEGETABLE TORTE

1 cup broccoli florets, blanched and shocked

1 cup cauliflower florets, blanched and shocked

2 zucchini (courgettes), sliced on the bias ¼-inch

2 yellow squash, sliced on the bias ¼-inch

Extra virgin olive oil

Salt and pepper to taste

2 large leeks, well cleaned and diced (white parts only)

2 red peppers, roasted and sliced

1 cup spinach, stems removed, blanched and shocked

MASHED POTATOES

4 large potatoes, peeled and boiled

Olive oil

Salt and pepper to taste

BASIL OIL

3 cups basil, blanched and shocked

3 cups extra virgin olive oil

Thanks to Chef David Burke, whose recipe appears in *Great Chefs Cook Vegan* by Linda Long. This gorgeous torte is an aesthetic and flavorful delight.

Preparation:

To make the Vegetable Torte: Set aside the blanched and shocked broccoli and cauliflower florets. Toss zucchini and squash with oil until well-coated and then season with salt and pepper. Grill on each side for 1 minute, do not mark; reserve warm. Sweat leeks in a little oil until tender and purée in a blender with about 2 tablespoons oil until smooth; reserve.

To make the Mashed Potatoes: Rice potatoes, or hand beat, or use low-speed setting on a mixer. Add oil until creamy. Season with salt and pepper; reserve warm.

To make the Basil Oil: Squeeze excess water from basil. Purée in a blender with oil until warm to the touch. Strain through double layers of cheesecloth and reserve for plating. NOTE: This will make more than needed for this recipe and can be used for other meals as a substitute for butter, pasta dishes, and seasoning for vegetables.

To make the Pommes Soufflés: Slice potatoes ⅛ to ¼-inch thick on a Japanese mandoline (a mandoline, which can be purchased at any kitchen supply store, is a kitchen utensil used for slicing and cutting raw vegetables). Rest in ice water for 30 minutes. Remove from water and with extreme care place potato slices in a pot of oil at 300 degrees F. Shake constantly and fry for 6 to 7 minutes. They should rise to the top after 5 minutes. (The ice-cold potatoes added to the hot oil will cause the potatoes to steam, brown, and soufflé.) Place the potatoes into a pot of oil at 400 degrees F to crisp. They will puff

(Continued on next page)

POMMES SOUFFLÉS

2 potatoes, peeled, shaped into an oval, and sliced on a mandoline

2 pots canola oil, 3-inches deep, one at 300 degrees F and the other at 400 F

12 ounces garden peas, blanched and reserved warm (frozen can be substituted)

up; continue to fry until golden brown. Be extremely careful as the hot oil will spit; drain. Serve, stuffed with peas as soon as torte is unmolded.

To assemble Torte: Grease a 2½ x 4-inch mold lightly with oil. Place on the dinner plate. For the base, press 3 zucchini slices and 3 squash slices into the mold with back of a spoon or a spatula. Follow with broccoli and cauliflower florets, followed by red pepper slices. Press ¼ cup spinach on top of peppers. Spoon leek purée over top. Fill mold to the top with Mashed Potatoes and flatten with a spatula. Bake in a 425 degree F oven for 10 minutes

How to plate: Carefully unmold Vegetable Torte onto a plate. Drizzle Basil Oil around the base and top with 3 Pomme Soufflés filled with garden peas. To save a step, skip making the Pomme Soufflés and simply line a row of nicely spaced peas around the top edge of the mashed potatoes. Serve immediately.

**Vegetable Carousel Torte
With Pommes Soufflés
Filled With Peas**

Photograph: Linda Long

Quinoa-Stuffed Acorn Squash With Cherries

Serves 4

❖ ❖ ❖ ❖ ❖ ❖ ❖ ❖ ❖ ❖

½–⅔ cups Eden Organic Quinoa, cooked (before cooking, rinse the grain until water runs clear in fine mesh sieve, then drain)

1 clove minced garlic

2 medium acorn squash, halved and seeded

½ cup walnuts, chopped

½ cup dried cherries

2 tablespoons brown rice syrup

½ teaspoon ground cinnamon

Organic safflower oil

This makes a beautiful, delicious and hearty Thanksgiving or winter holiday dish.

Preparation:

Pre-heat oven to 350 degrees F. Lightly oil the squash. Mix warm quinoa, brown rice syrup, walnuts, cherries, and cinnamon. Stuff each squash half with the mixture. Bake in a covered dish 45 minutes or until squash is tender. Top with a little vegan margarine, salt and pepper.

Ratatouille With Butternut Squash

Serves 6

❖ ❖ ❖ ❖ ❖ ❖ ❖ ❖ ❖ ❖ ❖ ❖

⅓ cup olive oil

2 medium onions, halved and thinly sliced to yield 2 ½ cups

1 teaspoon cumin seed

1 teaspoon ground coriander

2 teaspoons sea salt, more as needed

1 garlic clove, peeled and minced

1 eggplant, quarter lengthwise and thinly slice to yield 6 ½ cups. Place in colander, sprinkle with salt and leave for at least 30 minutes. Then press slices with your hands and blot with towels.

1 butternut squash, peeled, seeded, quartered lengthwise and thinly sliced to yield 5 cups

2 medium zucchini (courgettes), trimmed and sliced into rounds to yield 2 cups

1 yellow bell pepper, cored and sliced into strips to yield 1 ½ cups

One 28-ounce can diced tomatoes

Ratatouille is a vegetable stew that originated in France. That might explain why a crusty French bread is the perfect accompaniment.

Preparation:
Place a large, wide pan over medium heat, and add oil. When it's hot, add onions, cumin, coriander and 2 teaspoons salt. Sauté until onion is tender, about 3 minutes. Add garlic and sauté for 1 minute.

Add eggplant and squash. Cook, stirring occasionally, until they begin to soften, 3 to 4 minutes. Add zucchini, bell pepper and tomatoes. Stir well, and reduce heat to low. Simmer, partially covered and stirring occasionally, for 1 hour.

Remove from heat, and adjust salt to taste. Allow to cool to room temperature before serving. If desired, cover and refrigerate, reheating gently before serving. Serve with couscous.

Cauliflower Steak With Quinoa

Serves 4

❖ ❖ ❖ ❖ ❖ ❖ ❖ ❖ ❖ ❖ ❖ ❖

2 large heads cauliflower, cut into 1-inch-thick steaks

Olive oil for coating and sautéing

Salt and pepper to taste

1 cup quinoa

1 ½ cups vegetable stock, divided

2 shallots, sliced

1 leek, rinsed and sliced (white part only)

1 small apple, peeled and diced

1 clove garlic, finely chopped

½ cup zucchini (courgettes) in ¼-inch dice

1 teaspoon finely chopped fresh thyme leaves

1 tablespoon finely chopped chives

BASIL OIL
  2 cups well-washed basil leaves

  1 cup grapeseed oil, chilled

Thanks to Chef Dan Barber whose recipe appears in *Great Chefs Cook Vegan* by Linda Long. This creative and delicious recipe brings together flavorful cauliflower and nutty quinoa. The fresh herbs and apple make this dish sensational.

Preparation:
At the largest part of each cauliflower head, cut two cross-sections to create two 1-inch-thick steaks. In a large sauté pan coated with oil, brown the cauliflower steaks until golden brown on each side. Season with salt and pepper and set aside.

Over medium-low heat, sweat quinoa in 1 tablespoon oil until a nutty aroma is achieved. Turn off heat and add 1 cup stock; simmer until almost dry. Cover and let stand for 15 minutes. Fluff with a fork and set aside.

Cut remaining cauliflower into small florets and blanch in salted water until tender. Drain and spread florets on a baking sheet and place in a 300 degree F oven for about 15 minutes, or until florets have dried.

In a sauté pan, gently sweat the shallots, leek, apple, and garlic. Add the cauliflower florets and season with salt and pepper. Remove from heat, place in blender, and purée. (You will only need a few teaspoons for this recipe. The remaining purée can be frozen or thinned with stock for a cauliflower soup.)

In a large sauté pan coated with oil, sauté zucchini until slightly golden brown. Add quinoa and remaining vegetable stock. Season with salt and pepper to taste. Add 2 teaspoons cauliflower purée to thicken, add thyme and chives, and drizzle with oil.

To make the Basil Oil: Blanch basil and then shock in ice water; dry leaves well. In a blender, purée basil and grapeseed oil; strain.

How to plate: Place cauliflower steak on bed of quinoa and zucchini mixture and drizzle Basil Oil around the plate.

Cauliflower Steak With Quinoa

Photograph: Linda Long

Spicy Barbecued Tofu Triangles

Serves 6

❖ ❖ ❖ ❖ ❖ ❖ ❖ ❖ ❖ ❖ ❖

2 blocks extra-firm tofu

6 tablespoons extra virgin olive oil

¼ cup apple cider vinegar

2 tablespoons fresh lime juice

¾ cup tamari or soy sauce

¼ cup tomato sauce

1 large chipotle chile, canned in adobo sauce

6 tablespoons pure maple syrup

2 tablespoons ground cumin

2 tablespoons water

Pinch cayenne pepper

This recipe was originally published in Bryant Terry's book *Grub: Ideas for an Urban Organic Kitchen* (Tarcher/Penguin, 2006). This barbecue sauce is delicious, combining a bit of heat with a bit of sweet.

Preparation:

Pre-heat oven to 350 degrees F.

Place each tofu block on its side and cut into thirds. Keep the layers together, cut the tofu diagonally to make six long triangles, then cut the triangles down the middle to make 12 smaller triangles. Place each triangle between paper towels and press.

Warm 3 tablespoons of the olive oil in a large nonstick skillet over medium heat. Fry the tofu triangles in a snug layer, until golden brown, 7 to 10 minutes on each side. Depending on size of pan, you may need to cook in more than one batch. Drain on paper towels.

In a blender, combine the vinegar, lime juice, tamari, tomato sauce, chile, 3 tablespoons olive oil, maple syrup, cumin, water, and cayenne. Purée for 30 seconds.

Place the tofu in a large baking dish and cover with the marinade. Tightly cover the dish with foil. Bake for 1 hour, turning once halfway through.

Transfer the tofu and remaining marinade to a serving plate and serve with extra sauce to spoon on top.

Irish Stew

Serves 4

❖ ❖ ❖ ❖ ❖ ❖ ❖ ❖ ❖ ❖ ❖ ❖

1 pound seitan, cut into small cubes

3 tablespoons cornstarch

2 to 3 tablespoons canola oil

1 onion, sliced in half-moons

1 to 2 cloves garlic, minced

2 carrots, thick slices

2 parsnips, thick slices

1 sweet potato, cut into 1-inch cubes

1 Yukon Gold potato, cut into 1-inch cubes

8 Baby Bella mushrooms, sliced

1 teaspoon dried rosemary

1 teaspoon dried thyme

2 tablespoons unbleached white flour

3 tablespoons tamari

2 tablespoons tahini

2 to 3 cups water

Crushed black pepper

Sea salt to taste

Thanks to Mary Lawrence, a personal vegan chef in Connecticut, for this perfect winter meal that's easy to prepare and tastes great the next day. The seitan chunks are hearty enough to satisfy non-vegetarians that vegans are onto something big.

Preparation:

In a large bowl, toss seitan chunks with cornstarch and crushed black pepper until lightly coated. Pour 2 tablespoons oil into a large soup pot and heat on medium-high. Brown seitan chunks for 5 minutes on each side. Remove from pot, then deglaze the pot (release juices that have browned on the bottom) with mushrooms, onions and garlic, to sauté until soft. Add the remaining vegetables, rosemary, thyme and 2 to 3 cups of water. Bring to a boil, then simmer until vegetables are soft (20 to 30 minutes). In a small bowl, stir together tamari, flour and about ½ cup of water to form a thin paste. Stir this into the soup pot and heat until sauce thickens. Remove pot from heat and, forming a well in the center, stir in the tahini and gradually incorporate it into the sauce. Add seitan chunks to stew and simmer 5 minutes before serving.

Pasta

**Spaghetti With
Eggplant and Tomatoes**

Photograph: Linda Long

Spaghetti With Eggplant and Tomatoes

Serves 3 to 4

❖ ❖ ❖ ❖ ❖ ❖ ❖ ❖ ❖ ❖

Extra virgin olive oil as needed (figure at least ½ cup or more)

Several medium-sized eggplants (about 1 pound total)

Salt and freshly ground black pepper

4 cloves garlic, peeled and bruised*

2 or 3 dried chiles

3 cups chopped tomatoes

3 to 8 basil leaves, shredded

1 pound spaghetti or other long pasta

Chopped parsley for garnish

Adapted from a recipe created by Mark Bittman, author and food columnist for *The New York Times,* this elegant pasta sauce is out of this world. Serve with a salad of fresh, organic greens and you've got a perfect meal. *Buon appetito!*

Preparation:

Slice the eggplant about ½-inch thick, salt the slices and let them sit in a colander for about 30 minutes. Pat them dry and fry them a few pieces at a time in hot olive oil without crowding, adding more oil as needed. You will have to cook in batches unless you have a very large pan. Take your time and keep the heat fairly low; cook until really browned and soft. Remove to a plate (do not drain on paper towels).

Start water for pasta and salt it. Add a little more oil if needed to the same pan in which you cooked the eggplant, and turn the heat to medium-low (let the pan cool a bit if necessary). Bruise the garlic and discard the peel. Put it in the pan with the chiles and cook the garlic until lightly browned; you can press garlic a little more with the back of your spoon. Add the tomatoes, some salt and cook until saucy but not too dry, stirring occasionally. About 5 minutes before it's done add the basil you've shredded by cutting it with scissors.

Cook the pasta until done. Cut the eggplant, now cool, into strips. Drain the pasta but leave it a little wet. Toss in the saucepan with the tomato sauce and eggplant. Add salt and pepper as needed; add the parsley.

* To bruise garlic, lay it on a flat surface and place the flat side of a chef's knife atop it. Bump the flat part of the blade with the palm of your hand to crack open the clove to allow its juices to exude.

Lemon Pasta

Serves 4

❖ ❖ ❖ ❖ ❖ ❖ ❖ ❖ ❖ ❖ ❖

1 pound bow-tie or angel hair pasta

½ cup extra virgin olive oil

1 lemon zested

Juice from 2 lemons

½ cup chopped scallions

¼ cup chopped fresh parsley

¼ cup asparagus tips

½ cup pine nuts

½ cup chopped, fresh tomatoes

Coarse sea salt and freshly ground black pepper

Great thanks to Pamela Starr McKenna for adapting this lovely recipe from *The Summer Book* by Susan Branch.

Preparation:
In a steamer set over boiling water, steam asparagus tips about 3 minutes, until crisp-tender. Transfer asparagus to a colander and rinse under cool water. Drain asparagus well.

Cook pasta and drain well. Combine the rest of the ingredients and toss well with pasta in a large bowl. Season with salt and pepper. Serve hot or cold.

Linguine With Mushroom Sauce

Serves 3 to 4

❖ ❖ ❖ ❖ ❖ ❖ ❖ ❖ ❖ ❖ ❖

3 tablespoons extra virgin olive oil

3 cloves garlic, peeled and bruised*

1 small Vidalia onion, chopped

1 pound cremini mushrooms, finely chopped in food processor

2 tablespoons tomato paste

1 tablespoon black olive paste (tapenade)

⅓ cup dry red wine

1 teaspoon dried oregano

Salt and freshly ground black pepper

12 ounces linguine

Because it's quick, you *can* still make this pasta and heavenly sauce after a long, hard day at work.

Preparation:
Heat 2 tablespoons olive oil in a large skillet. Add garlic and onion and sauté a couple of minutes until soft. Add mushrooms and cook over medium heat until they wilt and release their juices. Do not let juices evaporate. Stir in tomato paste and tapenade. Add wine, cook briefly then season with oregano, salt and pepper. Remove from heat.

Bring a pot of salted water to a boil, add linguine stir and cook about 3 minutes. Drain. Transfer linguine to skillet. Add remaining oil. Cook, gently folding ingredients together, until mushroom mixture has reheated and is evenly mixed with linguine

*To bruise garlic, lay it on a flat surface and place the flat side of a chef's knife atop it. Bump the flat part of the blade with the palm of your hand to crack open the clove to allow its juices to exude.

Linguine With Raw Nut Pesto and Tomato Sauce

Serves 4

❖ ❖ ❖ ❖ ❖ ❖ ❖ ❖ ❖ ❖ ❖

TOMATO SAUCE

¼ cup olive oil

1 small onion, finely chopped

2 shallots, finely chopped

1 clove garlic, finely chopped

1 pound (about 2 cups) canned whole peeled tomatoes, with juice

Salt and freshly ground black pepper

PESTO

2 garlic cloves, crushed

2 teaspoons hot red pepper flakes

5 tablespoons extra virgin olive oil

2 cups mixed whole raw nuts, such as pine nuts, walnuts, pistachios

3 to 4 leaves of fresh mint

Freshly ground black pepper

LINGUINE

Salt

1 pound linguine

Fresh mint leaves, for garnish

Grated vegan parmesan

In this lightly spiced and aromatic pasta sauce, nuts are the meat of the matter.

Preparation:

To make tomato sauce, use a heavy-based saucepan over medium heat to heat oil and sauté onion and shallots until translucent. Add garlic and tomatoes with their juices, breaking up the tomatoes with a wooden spoon. Season with salt and pepper to taste. Simmer uncovered until most of the juices have evaporated, 20 to 30 minutes. Meanwhile, prepare pesto.

For the pesto, use a food processor, combine garlic, hot pepper flakes, olive oil, nuts and mint. Pulse to make a smooth paste (a slightly coarse nut butter). Season with black pepper to taste and set aside.

Bring a large pot of lightly salted water to a boil. Add linguine and cook until al dente (firm to the bite). Set aside ½ cup pasta water, and drain pasta well. Return pasta to the warm pot and add pesto and tomato sauce. Toss well to coat, adding reserved water as needed to thin the sauce. Transfer to a warm serving bowl and garnish with fresh mint leaves. Serve with vegan parmesan passed separately.

Mediterranean Pasta With Garlic, Greens and Butter Beans

Serves 4 to 6

❖ ❖ ❖ ❖ ❖ ❖ ❖ ❖ ❖ ❖

1 pound fusilli pasta, cooked and drained

½ cup calamata olives, sliced in half

¼ cup sundried tomatoes, diced

½ cup artichoke hearts

1 can of butter beans, drained and rinsed

1 large bunch of greens, blanched and chopped

¼ cup olive oil

2 to 3 cloves garlic, crushed

Salt and pepper to taste

Fresh chopped parsley

1 to 2 tablespoons nutritional yeast

Mary Lawrence, personal vegan chef and owner of Well on Wheels® of Connecticut, offers this simple pasta dish enriched by butter beans and enlivened by greens. Almost any type of greens will work in this recipe, but a big bunch of collards will have an assertive flavor and substance.

Preparation:
Sauté garlic in olive oil until fragrant. Stir in greens, sundried tomatoes, olives, beans and artichokes. Toss with pasta and season with nutritional yeast, salt and pepper. Garnish with fresh parsley.

Pasta With Basil Pesto, White Beans and Zucchini

Serves 4 to 6

❖ ❖ ❖ ❖ ❖ ❖ ❖ ❖ ❖ ❖ ❖

4 cups diced zucchini (courgettes), with seeds scraped away if using very large zucchini

4 cups loosely packed basil leaves

2 to 4 cloves garlic (divided)

¼ cup pine nuts

½ cup extra virgin olive oil, plus 2 to 3 tablespoons for sauté

1 pound short pasta (gemelli or penne will work well)

Salt, pepper and crushed red pepper flakes, to taste

2 (15-ounce) cans small white beans

Vegan parmesan substitute or toasted bread crumbs

Thanks to Trish Sebben-Krupka for this delicious pesto pasta. Serve with fresh greens and warm bread.

Preparation:

Toast pine nuts in oven or sauté pan until lightly browned. Set aside to cool a bit while you prepare remaining ingredients.

Place basil, one or two cloves of garlic, and pine nuts in food processor or blender and pulse a few times. With the machine running, slowly pour in olive oil. Stir in salt and freshly ground pepper to taste. Set aside, covered, while you bring the pasta water to a boil.

When pasta water begins to boil, salt the water generously, return to a full rolling boil, add your pasta and stir well.

Meanwhile, chop one or two cloves of garlic finely. Heat 2 to 3 tablespoons of oil in a large sauté pan. Add garlic and sauté until fragrant and lightly browned. Add zucchini, season with salt, pepper, and crushed red pepper flakes, and sauté until crisp-tender. Add white beans and a little bit of the pasta water; reduce heat to a simmer. When pasta is cooked al dente, reserve about ½ cup of cooking liquid, add pasta directly to sauté pan and toss for a minute or two over medium heat.

Remove to warm serving bowl, and stir in about half to three quarters of the pesto mixture (you can freeze any leftover pesto, or refrigerate and use within a day or so). If it looks dry, add a few tablespoons of the pasta water to loosen it up.

Garnish with vegan "parmesan" or toasted bread crumbs, freshly ground pepper, a drizzle of extra virgin olive oil, and a few sprigs of basil. Serve immediately.

Farfalle With Broccoli Rabe

Serves 4

❖ ❖ ❖ ❖ ❖ ❖ ❖ ❖ ❖ ❖ ❖

1 pound broccoli rabe

¼ cup extra virgin olive oil

3 large cloves garlic, peeled and crushed

1 pound farfalle (bow-tie) pasta, or penne

Pinch of red crushed red pepper flakes, or to taste

Sea salt to taste

Broccoli rabe (rapini) is a leafy mustard green closely related to turnips, not broccoli. It's a source of vitamins A, C and K as well as potassium. Boiling this green briefly before sautéing relieves it of excess bitterness.

Preparation:

Peel off the skin from any tough lower stalks of the rabe. Coarsely chop the rabe into 2-inch lengths, wash it and drain.

Bring a large, 6 quart pot of water to a boil, add 2 tablespoons salt and rabe. Cover partially and cook for 3 minutes after the water returns to a boil. Remove rabe with slotted spoon and drain in colander.

Meanwhile, place the olive oil in a large skillet over low heat. Add the garlic and sauté gently about 1 minute until it begins to sizzle.

Transfer drained rabe to the skillet. Turn the heat up to medium; stir, and cook until tender, about 3 to 5 minutes longer. Add red pepper flakes.

Meanwhile, bring water to a boil in a large pot. Add the pasta, 1 tablespoon salt; stir to prevent the pasta from sticking together, and cook until just al dente (tender but quite firm to the bite). Drain pasta, leaving some water clinging to the noodles. Add pasta to the skillet that contains the broccoli rabe, garlic and red paper flakes. Turn heat on low and toss quickly to coat and combine. Season with salt and freshly milled black pepper. Serve at once.

Risotto

Asparagus and Spring Pea Risotto

Photograph: Linda Long

Asparagus and Spring Pea Risotto

Serves 3 to 4

❖ ❖ ❖ ❖ ❖ ❖ ❖ ❖ ❖ ❖ ❖ ❖ ❖

1 ¾ cups fresh asparagus, peeled, trimmed and cut into 1-inch long pieces, tips reserved

1 ¼ cups shelled sweet peas (frozen, thawed peas are acceptable)

5 to 6 cups vegetable broth

3 tablespoons extra virgin olive oil

2 tablespoons vegan margarine

2 to 3 large shallots, minced

1 ½ cups Arborio risotto rice

½ cup dry white wine

Salt and pepper to taste

Patience is a virtue, as the adage goes. Making a risotto requires a bit—but the rewards are huge.

Preparation:

Bring a saucepan of water to a boil. Add the asparagus stalks and cook about 5 minutes until quite soft. Rinse quickly under cold water. Place cooked asparagus in a food processor and add just enough water to purée until almost smooth; set aside.

Cook half of the fresh peas for 3 to 4 minutes in boiling water. Add these peas to asparagus purée mixture, and allow machine to purée asparagus/pea mixture for a few seconds until mostly smooth.

Heat broth in a medium saucepan over low heat. Add olive oil and one tablespoon margarine in a large, heavy saucepan over medium heat. When heated, add shallots, stirring 3 to 5 minutes until softened.

Add rice to pan; stir the rice for about 2 to 3 minutes, until grains are well coated with oil, translucent, with a white dot in the centers. Add wine and stir until absorbed.

Add warmed broth, a ladleful at a time, stirring frequently, after each addition. Wait until broth is almost completely absorbed before adding more.

After about 15 minutes, add remaining asparagus tips, continuing to add broth when necessary. In 5 minutes, begin tasting the rice. When the rice is almost tender to the bite but slightly firm in the center and looks creamy, add remaining whole peas, and stir in asparagus-pea purée.

Heat for a few seconds. Remove skillet from heat, add remaining margarine and stir briskly. Season with salt and pepper.

Cauliflower Risotto

Serves 4

❖ ❖ ❖ ❖ ❖ ❖ ❖ ❖ ❖ ❖ ❖ ❖ ❖

1 head cauliflower

½ Vidalia onion, finely chopped

1 clove garlic, minced

2 tablespoons olive oil

2 tablespoons vegan margarine

1 cup Arborio risotto rice

4 cups vegetable broth

½ cup dry white wine

4 or more tablespoons toasted
bread crumbs (make your own,
see below)

In Western cooking, cauliflower is often relegated to the crudités platter. This warm, filling risotto gives it a completely new role.

Preparation:
Separate cauliflower florets from stems. Chop florets into 1-inch or less pieces. Finely chop stalks. Keep stalks and florets separate.

In large saucepan, sauté onion and garlic, along with finely chopped cauliflower stalks, in oil and margarine for 5 minutes until softened.

Add rice, stir and fry for 2 minutes, until opaque. Add ½ cup wine.

In another saucepan, bring broth to gentle boil and add the very small cauliflower florets.

Ladle broth only into rice, one ladleful at a time, stirring frequently, after each addition. Wait until broth is almost completely absorbed before adding more.

After about 10 minutes, when rice is half done, add softened cauliflower florets to rice mixture and gently squash each floret into rice as it is added. Continue to add broth when necessary.

After about 20 minutes in total when all broth is absorbed, take rice off heat and let sit without stirring for 1 minute.

Serve on plates and top with toasted bread crumbs made from whole grain bread that has been toasted in the toaster oven.

Caramelized Leek and Shiitake Risotto

Serves 4 to 6

❖ ❖ ❖ ❖ ❖ ❖ ❖ ❖ ❖ ❖ ❖ ❖

LEEKS

2 cups leeks, white and light green parts only, halved, well-rinsed in several changes of water, and thinly sliced

2 tablespoons olive oil

Salt and freshly ground pepper

MUSHROOMS

2 to 3 tablespoons olive oil

2 small shallots, finely chopped

2 cloves garlic, finely chopped

1 pound shiitake mushrooms, stemmed and thinly sliced

2 tablespoons dry white wine

2 tablespoons fresh parsley

Salt and freshly ground pepper

RISOTTO

1 tablespoon olive oil

2 small shallots, finely chopped

1½ cups Arborio rice

6 cups light vegetable stock, brought to a simmer

This remarkable risotto by Trish Sebben-Krupka is at its best with a salad of fresh leafy greens, followed by seasonal fruit for dessert.

Preparation:
In a small sauté pan, heat 2 tablespoons olive oil over medium heat. Add leeks and a little salt, and reduce the heat to low. Cook, stirring occasionally, until leeks are golden and caramelized. Set aside.

While leeks are caramelizing, prepare Parsley Oil Garnish by placing all ingredients into a blender or food processor. Blend until parsley is completely broken down and the mixture is bright green. Allow to rest for half an hour or so, and then strain into a small bowl. Cover surface with airtight wrap and set aside at room temperature until ready to serve. (Can be made one day in advance—keep well-covered and refrigerated.)

In a large sauté pan, heat 2 to 3 tablespoons of olive oil over medium-high heat. Add 2 finely chopped shallots and a pinch of salt and sauté for a few minutes, until shallots begin to soften. Add garlic and cook 1 minute more. Add mushrooms; sauté, stirring frequently, until mushrooms exude their liquid and begin to brown. Deglaze (release juices that have browned on the bottom of the pan) with white wine, season with fresh parsley, salt and pepper, and set aside in a bowl.

Wipe clean the pan in which you sautéed the mushrooms, and heat 1 tablespoon olive oil over medium heat. Bring vegetable stock to a simmer (adding cold stock will ruin the dish). Add the remaining 2 shallots, and sauté briefly, about 2 minutes. Add the rice all at once, and stir constantly until rice is opaque and lightly toasted (not browned). It will smell a little like fresh popcorn when it's ready.

PARSLEY OIL GARNISH
1 bunch fresh Italian parsley,
leaves only

½ cup extra virgin olive oil

Salt and freshly ground pepper

A drop or two of champagne or
white vinegar

Add 2 tablespoons dry white wine, and stir constantly until wine has evaporated.

Add half of the stock all at once, reduce heat to medium-low, and stir frequently until nearly all of the liquid has been absorbed into the rice. Add the mushroom and leek mixtures to the pan and stir well to combine.

Add the remaining stock, one ladleful at a time, stirring constantly as the rice releases its starches to form the creamy base for a perfect risotto. When nearly all of the stock has been added, taste frequently —you want to remove the risotto from the heat when it is still a little loose and *al dente,* or firm to the bite. This is important, as risotto will keep cooking once you remove it from the heat, so a risotto that seems done in the pan can easily become a thick, mushy mess on the plate.

Season with salt and freshly ground pepper, ladle immediately into warm bowls, and serve garnished with a tablespoon of the parsley oil per serving.

Fennel and Onion Risotto

Serves 4 to 6

❖ ❖ ❖ ❖ ❖ ❖ ❖ ❖ ❖ ❖ ❖ ❖

2 tablespoons extra virgin olive oil

4 to 5 cups vegetable broth

1 medium fennel bulb, chopped

½ Vidalia onion, chopped

4 cloves garlic, chopped

1 cup frozen, thawed peas

1 cup Arborio risotto rice

¼ cup white wine

1 tablespoons vegan margarine

Chopped Italian parsley for garnish

Fennel tastes like a cross between cabbage, celery and licorice. It's a popular vegetable in Italy, rich in Vitamin C.

Preparation:

Heat broth in a medium saucepan over low heat.

In large, heavy saucepan, heat olive oil, add onion and garlic. Sauté 3 to 5 minutes over medium heat.

Stir in the rice, cook 2 minutes until opaque. Add wine and stir until absorbed. Then add fennel.

Add warmed broth, a ladleful at a time, stirring frequently, after each addition. Wait until broth is almost completely absorbed before adding more.

After 20 minutes, add peas, Continue stirring for about 2 minutes as risotto becomes almost tender to the bite but slightly firm in the center and looks creamy. Then remove from heat, add 1 tablespoon margarine, stir, and season with salt and pepper. Garnish with chopped Italian parsley and serve.

Risotto, Milan Style

Serves 4

❖ ❖ ❖ ❖ ❖ ❖ ❖ ❖ ❖ ❖ ❖ ❖

5 tablespoons extra virgin olive oil

1 tablespoon soy margarine

1 large onion, diced

2 cloves of finely chopped garlic

¼ cup white wine

½ teaspoon saffron threads

1 cup Arborio rice

4 cups vegetable broth

Sea salt and freshly ground pepper

Italian Parsley, chopped as garnish

Saffron, although expensive, offers a wonderful, exotic taste and imparts a golden hue. Buy only threads, orange-red in tone.

Preparation:

Heat vegetable broth to a slow simmer in a saucepan.

In large saucepan, sauté onion and garlic in oil for 5 minutes until softened. Add rice, stir to coat well, keep stirring and cook 2 minutes, until opaque. Sprinkle in saffron threads, add wine and allow to be absorbed.

Ladle broth into rice, one ladleful at a time, stirring frequently over medium heat, after each addition. Wait until broth is almost completely absorbed before adding more. Continue this process for about 20 minutes, until broth is absorbed, rice is tender but al dente, firm to the bite.

Take rice off heat, add freshly ground pepper, salt if needed, the tablespoon of margarine and mix thoroughly. Let it sit without stirring for 1 or 2 minutes and serve garnished with chopped parsley.

If desired, sprinkle cooked risotto with vegan parmesan.

Zucchini Risotto

❖ ❖ ❖ ❖ ❖ ❖ ❖ ❖ ❖ ❖ ❖

3 to 4 medium zucchini

½ cup chopped Vidalia onion

5 tablespoons extra virgin olive oil

2 cloves garlic, finely chopped

¼ cup white wine

5 cups vegetable broth

2 tablespoons soy margarine

1½ cups Arborio rice

Sea salt and freshly ground black pepper

1 tablespoon finely chopped Italian parsley

Zucchini—courgettes in Britain and New Zealand—are an abundant summer squash, often seen relegated to a side dish. This delicate risotto, however, brings this tender squash center stage.

Preparation:
Wash zucchini and slice into chunks ½-inch thick. Set aside.

In large skillet, sauté onion in 3 tablespoons of oil about 5 minutes over medium heat. When the onion becomes translucent, add the garlic, stir and cook several seconds and then add the zucchini and turn the heat down to medium-low. Add a very small pinch of salt after 10 minutes. The zucchini are done in about 30 minutes, after they've turned a golden color.

Heat vegetable broth to a slow simmer in a medium saucepan.

Transfer the zucchini to a heavy saucepan, leaving behind in the skillet as much of the cooking oil as possible. Add 1 tablespoon of oil and 2 tablespoons of margarine to the saucepan and turn the heat to medium-high. When the oil and zucchini begin to bubble, add the rice and stir to coat well, cooking and stirring about 1 to 2 minutes, until rice is opaque. Add wine and allow to be absorbed.

Ladle broth into rice, one ladleful at a time, stirring frequently over medium heat, after each addition. Wait until broth is almost completely absorbed before adding more. Continue this process for about 20 minutes, until broth is absorbed, rice is tender but *al dente*—firm to the bite.

Turn off heat, add freshly ground pepper, salt if needed, the remaining tablespoon of oil, the chopped parsley, and mix thoroughly. Let it sit without stirring for a 1 or 2 minutes and serve.

Vegetables and Side Dishes

Succotash

Photograph: Linda Long

Succotash

Serves 6 or more

❖ ❖ ❖ ❖ ❖ ❖ ❖ ❖ ❖ ❖ ❖

4 cups fresh corn (about 6 to 8 ears)

2 cups small, shelled fresh lima beans

2 cups fresh string beans, cut into 1-inch pieces

¼ pound vegan margarine

4 scallions, trimmed

2 to 3 tablespoons non-dairy creamer

A staple of childhood re-imagined. A hearty side dish worthy of second and third helpings.

Preparation:

Husk the corn and remove all the silk. With a sharp knife, remove the kernels from the cob, slicing from the top of the ear downward and not too close to the cob. With a small spoon, scrape the pulp from the cobs into a mixing bowl. Add the kernels and reserve.

In a medium-sized pot of lightly salted boiling water, blanch the lima beans until they are almost tender, then cool under cold water. Reserve and repeat the process with the string beans.

In a large heavy saucepan, melt the margarine over medium heat. Add the corn and its juice, and cook for 10 minutes, stirring often.

Slice the scallions into ½-inch pieces, including some of the green, and set aside. Add both types of beans to the corn and cook for another 10 minutes, stirring often. After 5 minutes, add the scallions and fold in the creamer to loosen the mixture. Spoon the succotash into a warm serving bowl. Serve immediately.

Mashed Potatoes With Celery Root

Serves 4 to 6

❖ ❖ ❖ ❖ ❖ ❖ ❖ ❖ ❖ ❖ ❖ ❖

2 pounds Yukon Gold potatoes, peeled

1 celery root, about 1 pound, peeled

½–¾ cup hot vegetable broth

3 tablespoons soy margarine

½ teaspoon salt

Ground black pepper

Garnish with snipped fresh chives

Sometimes the tried and true is in need of reinvention—a little something new. Celery root brings this ever-popular and ever-versatile side dish to new heights. Luscious.

Preparation:
Cut the potatoes and celery root into large pieces. If more than a few minutes will pass between peeling the celery root and cooking it, cover it in a bath of cold water and 1 tablespoon of lemon juice to keep it from discoloring.

Put potatoes and celery root in a saucepan, cover with cold salted water, and bring to a boil. Simmer until tender, about 20 minutes. Drain and return the vegetables to the pan. Over low heat, mash the vegetables and beat with a hand-held mixer, adding vegetable broth, margarine, salt and pepper. Blend until smooth.

Stir in snipped fresh chives or chopped parsley before serving.

Herbed Couscous

Serves 6

❖ ❖ ❖ ❖ ❖ ❖ ❖ ❖ ❖ ❖ ❖ ❖

1 teaspoon vegetable stock granules or 1 teaspoon crumbled vegetable bouillon cube

1 ½ cups water

1 ½ cups couscous

½ cup finely chopped parsley

½ cup finely sliced scallions

2 tablespoons olive oil

Salt

Couscous is pasta, not a grain as is commonly thought—and it's eaten all over the world, in a wide variety of ways. This side dish is a perfect accompaniment to any soup or stew.

Preparation:
In a small saucepan, combine 1½ cups water and vegetable stock granules. Bring to a simmer, then remove from heat, and stir to dissolve granules. Add couscous, cover and set aside until water is absorbed, about 10 minutes.

Fluff couscous with a fork. Mix in parsley and scallions and add oil, working it through with a fork to mix well. Season with salt to taste, and serve.

Mango Rice

❖ ❖ ❖ ❖ ❖ ❖ ❖ ❖ ❖ ❖ ❖ ❖

BASMATI RICE

1 cup long-grained basmati rice (rinse rice ahead of time—and soak in water ½ hour; when cooking, let water boil then add rice; do not stir)

4 tablespoons raw peanuts

2 to 3 curry leaves

MASALA

1 ½ teaspoons brown mustard seeds

½ teaspoon asafetida powder

3 red chiles, fresh or dried

½ teaspoon turmeric powder

4 tablespoons coconut, fresh-grated

1 ½ cups green mango, fresh-grated

FOR TEMPERING

3 tablespoons grapeseed oil

1 teaspoon brown mustard seed

1 tablespoon chana dal, picked and rinsed

½ red chili, halved

2 to 3 curry leaves

Thanks to California Chef Matt Murray for this delicious recipe. This recipe calls for curry leaves—which must not be mistaken for curry powder. Fresh curry leaves can often be found at Asian grocery stores and the dried variety can be found in well-stocked health food stores and co-ops, often in the bulk herbs section.

Preparation:
Cook the rice and spread on a platter to cool.

To prepare the Masala: Peel off the green skin of the mango and discard. Then grate the yellow-orange flesh. Place mustard seeds, asafetida powder, three red chilies, ground turmeric and grated coconut in a blender with half of the grated mango. Blend into a fine paste.

For tempering: Heat the oil in a heavy-bottomed pan; add mustard seeds, dal, chili, and three curry leaves. When the seeds sputter, add the peanuts. Once dal is golden, add the remaining mango. Sauté for a few minutes over medium heat, until the mango is cooked. Now add the masala and cook until the raw smell disappears.

Stir the mixture into cooled rice with remaining curry leaves.

Roasted Balsamic Potatoes and Onions

Serves 4

❖ ❖ ❖ ❖ ❖ ❖ ❖ ❖ ❖ ❖ ❖ ❖

2 tablespoons olive oil

1¼–1½ pounds red potatoes, halved (or cut in 1-inch chunks)

¾ pound onions, peeled leaving root ends intact, cut into ¾-inch wedges

¼ cup balsamic vinegar

1 tablespoon fresh thyme or 1 teaspoon dried

½ teaspoon salt

½ teaspoon pepper

These roasted potatoes, truly, are great with anything. The balsamic and thyme give them mouth-watering appeal.

Preparation:
Pre-heat oven to 400 degrees F. Pour oil into a 10½ x 15½-inch (jellyroll) pan. Add the potatoes and onions and toss to coat with oil. Cover with foil and roast for 30 minutes. Remove the foil. Increase heat to 450 degrees F. Add remaining ingredients and toss thoroughly. Continue to roast, tossing occasionally for 30 to 40 minutes, or until vegetables are browned and potatoes are crisp on the edges.

Irish Mashed Potatoes With Greens

Serves 6

❖ ❖ ❖ ❖ ❖ ❖ ❖ ❖ ❖ ❖ ❖ ❖

2 to 3 pounds Yukon Gold potatoes, peeled and cubed

2 parsnips, peeled and sliced

1 cup kale, stems removed and coarsely chopped

⅔ cup vanilla rice milk

4 tablespoons vegan margarine

3 thinly sliced scallions

Salt and pepper to taste

Thanks to Mary Lawrence, the owner of Well on Wheels®, Connecticut's premiere vegan personal chef service. This is a great way to sneak in your greens! Everybody loves mashed potatoes, and you will be pleasantly surprised at how delicious and unassuming kale can be when served this way.

Preparation:
Boil potatoes and parsnips 15 to 20 minutes or until fork tender. Drain and mash potatoes and parsnips, then stir together with rice milk and margarine until fluffy. In a separate pot of boiling water, blanch chopped kale and scallions until wilted (about 30 seconds). Drain and pour cold water over kale and scallions, then combine with mashed potatoes and parsnips. Add salt and pepper to taste.

Baby Artichokes Provençal Style

Serves 2 to 4

❖ ❖ ❖ ❖ ❖ ❖ ❖ ❖ ❖ ❖ ❖ ❖

¼ cup extra virgin olive oil

4 cloves garlic, peeled, then crushed

Fresh thyme or rosemary, optional

½ cup flavorful black olives, pitted

Salt

12 little (or baby) artichokes

1 pint grape tomatoes, halved or left whole, or about 1 ½ cups any other tomatoes, chopped

Chopped fresh parsley leaves for garnish.

Thanks to Mark Bittman, Author of *How to Cook Everything Vegetarian* and food columnist at *The New York Times*, for sharing this recipe.

Preparation:
Combine oil and garlic in a large skillet (cast iron is good), over medium-low heat. When garlic sizzles, add herb, olives and a pinch of salt.

Meanwhile, prepare artichokes: remove hard leaves, then cut off spiky end, about 1-inch down from top; trim bottoms, cut artichokes in half. Immediately put the cleaned artichokes into a large ceramic or glass bowl of cold water to which you have added the juice of 1 lemon. Leave them in the water until you are ready to fry them.

Next drain the artichokes and dry them thoroughly. Add them to pan as they are ready, cut side down. When about half of them are in pan, raise heat so they brown a bit; move them around as you add remaining artichokes so that they brown evenly.

When artichokes brown, add tomatoes and a splash of water. Cover until artichokes are tender, 10 to 20 minutes. Add water if needed. Adjust seasoning, garnish and serve hot or at room temperature.

**Baby Artichokes
Provençal Style**

Photograph: Jane Seymour

Fried Zucchini Blossoms

For every six to eight zucchini blossoms, you will need:

❖ ❖ ❖ ❖ ❖ ❖ ❖ ❖ ❖ ❖

1½ teaspoons Ener-g egg replacer

2 tablespoons warm water

A pinch each of salt and pepper

¼ cup Italian-seasoned bread crumbs

¼ cup grapeseed oil, for frying

Trish Sebben-Krupka's grandfather, Angelo Sebben, spent the first sixteen years of his life on a farm in the Northern Italian town of Fonzaso. Trish says, "At 87, he still enjoys his small garden and can grow anything you can think of, so when we need gardening advice, we call Pop! My husband Jim and I enjoy tending our plants and carrying on this tradition as much as we love eating and sharing the fruits of our labor, but we had a difficult time growing zucchini until Pop advised planting two of them together in a four-foot square patch, picking often, and removing the male flowers that don't produce a 'zucchino.'"

If you don't have a garden, try your local farmers' market, as squash blossoms are readily available by the bagful throughout the summer. Pick early in the morning, when flowers are open, and store in a paper bag in the fridge for a few hours if necessary.

Preparation:
Carefully remove the stamen from the center of each blossom by pinching it between your thumb and forefinger, and rinse gently under cool water. Heat oil in a fry pan until shimmering and very hot, but not smoking.

Meanwhile, whisk egg replacer, water, and a little salt and pepper in a small bowl. Place bread crumbs in another bowl. Dip each blossom first in your vegan egg wash and then in breadcrumbs, and place immediately into hot oil. Pan fry, turning once, until crispy and golden. Sprinkle with salt and enjoy immediately!

Quinoa With Pine Nuts

Serves 3 to 4

❖ ❖ ❖ ❖ ❖ ❖ ❖ ❖ ❖ ❖ ❖ ❖

½ cup Vidalia or yellow onions, chopped fine

2 tablespoons extra virgin olive oil

1 tablespoon sesame oil

2 cloves minced garlic

¾ cup quinoa (rinse until water runs clear in fine mesh sieve; then drain)

1½ cups vegetable broth

½ teaspoon thyme

3 to 4 tablespoons toasted pine nuts

Salt and pepper to taste

Quinoa originated in South America where it has been a staple for 6,000 years. It also happens to be incredibly good for you—with its high fiber, protein and mineral content. Oh, it also happens to be delectable.

Preparation:
Sauté onion and garlic in saucepan with oils, stirring for several minutes until onion starts to look opaque.

Turn the heat up to medium-high, add the rinsed and drained quinoa. Stir a couple of minutes as the grains start toasting. Add salt, pepper, thyme and broth; cover and reduce heat to low. Cook covered 15 to 20 minutes until liquid is absorbed.

Sprinkle with toasted pine nuts and serve.

Sautéed Broccoli With Garlic and Pine Nuts

Serves 3

❖ ❖ ❖ ❖ ❖ ❖ ❖ ❖ ❖ ❖

1 head broccoli (about 1½ pounds)

Salt

2 teaspoons finely chopped garlic

¼ cup extra virgin olive oil

¼–⅓ cup pine nuts, lightly toasted

Sometimes simple is the way to go. Pine nuts and garlic bring out the best in broccoli.

Preparation:

Wash and trim the broccoli, cutting each head into separate, but not-too-small florets. Discard the stalks.

Bring water to boil with 1 teaspoon salt in large saucepan. Add the florets and boil until almost tender, about 4 to 5 minutes, depending on the freshness of the broccoli. Drain and set aside.

In a skillet, sauté the garlic in olive oil over medium heat. When the garlic colors lightly, add the broccoli, about 1 teaspoon of salt, and sauté lightly for about 1 minute, turning broccoli.

Add the toasted pine nuts to the pan, toss together and serve at once.

Grilled Polenta With Corn

Serves 6

❖ ❖ ❖ ❖ ❖ ❖ ❖ ❖ ❖ ❖ ❖ ❖

1 tablespoon olive oil

1 small onion, finely chopped

1 garlic clove, minced

1 cup frozen or fresh corn kernels

3 cups water, divided

1 teaspoon salt

1 cup stone-ground cornmeal

Additional olive oil

You can add just about anything to this versatile polenta. Instead of corn kernels, you may want to use sun-dried tomatoes, potatoes, peppers—or whatever you choose!

Preparation:

Heat 1 tablespoon oil in medium skillet over medium heat. Add onion, sauté 5 minutes. Add garlic, sauté 1 minute. Add corn, sauté until heated through, about 3 minutes. Remove from heat.

Bring 2 cups water and 1 teaspoon salt to boil in medium saucepan over medium heat. Whisk cornmeal and 1 cup water in medium bowl to blend. Whisk cornmeal-water mixture into boiling water and cook over low heat. Cook until polenta is smooth and thick, stirring often, about 30 minutes. Stir in the corn mixture.

Brush 11x7x2-inch dish with oil. Spread polenta in dish. Cool completely. (Can be made one day ahead. Cover and chill.)

Prepare barbecue (medium-high heat). Brush grill with oil. Cut polenta into 12 squares. Brush both sides with oil. Place on grill, cover grill. Grill until polenta is golden brown, about 3 minutes per side. Serve hot.

Yellow Squash and Zucchini With Herbs

Serves 3 to 4

❖ ❖ ❖ ❖ ❖ ❖ ❖ ❖ ❖ ❖ ❖

2 small, fresh, firm yellow summer squash (6-inch in length and 1 to 1½ - inches in diameter)

2 small, fresh, firm zucchini

2 tablespoons extra virgin olive oil

1 small, yellow onion, chopped

2 cloves garlic, peeled and bruised*

½ teaspoon salt, or to taste

3 tablespoons water

1 teaspoon dried basil

1½ teaspoons chopped fresh parsley

Freshly ground black pepper

Squash and zucchini (courgettes) are versatile, nutritious and delicious. This easy and fast recipe makes a remarkable side dish that goes with practically anything.

Preparation:

Slice the squash crosswise about ¼-inch thick. Set aside.

Add the olive oil to a skillet over medium heat. Add the onion and garlic and sauté a couple of minutes. Add the squashes and salt and stir while adding basil and parsley.

Reduce the heat to medium-low and add the water. Stir and partially cover, cooking until tender about 10 minutes, while stirring occasionally.

Add black pepper to taste and more salt, if desired. Serve immediately.

*To bruise garlic, lay it on a flat surface and place the flat side of a chef's knife atop it. Bump the flat part of the blade with the palm of your hand to crack open the clove to allow its juices to flow.

Pancakes, Breads and Muffins

**Chocolate-Stuffed
Michigan French Toast**

Photograph: Linda Long

Chocolate-Stuffed Michigan French Toast

Serves 4

❖ ❖ ❖ ❖ ❖ ❖ ❖ ❖ ❖ ❖ ❖ ❖

STRAWBERRY-PEACH COMPOTE

1 cup fresh peaches, cut into wedges

1 cup quartered fresh strawberries

2 tablespoons brown sugar

DIPPING BATTER

2 cups vanilla soy milk

1 cup freshly squeezed orange juice

6 tablespoons Grand Marnier liqueur

2 teaspoons ground cinnamon

2 tablespoons egg replacer (Red Mill or Ener-G)

4 tablespoons maple syrup

CHOCOLATE-STUFFED FRENCH TOAST

12 slices bread (your choice—but slightly dry is preferable)

12 squares organic bittersweet chocolate

4 cups Rice Krispies

½ cup powdered sugar

Thanks to Chef Josef Huber whose recipe appears in *Great Chefs Cook Vegan* by Linda Long. This decadent French toast would certainly make an impressive and mouth-watering Sunday morning brunch item. If you are looking for something faster, you could also forgo the compote and serve with vegan butter and maple syrup.

Preparation:

To make the Strawberry-Peach Compote: Place all compote ingredients into a small saucepan over low heat and bring to a simmer for about 10 minutes. Check to make sure peaches are soft and not crunchy. Remove from heat and cool in refrigerator.

To make the Dipping Batter: Prepare the batter by whisking together the soy milk, orange juice, Grand Marnier, cinnamon, egg replacer, and maple syrup. Pour the batter into a pan large enough to accommodate the bread slices.

To make the Chocolate-Stuffed French Toast: Place a chocolate square on 12 bread slices. Take the other bread slices and place them on top of the chocolate slices like a sandwich. Place the "sandwich" slices in the Dipping Batter and let soak for 20 seconds, turning them over after 10 seconds or so. Place Rice Krispies in a bowl, and then coat the bread slices with Rice Krispies.

Heat a griddle or sauté pan over medium heat and coat with vegetable spray. Place the sandwiches on the hot griddle and cook until the bottom turns golden brown; flip and cook on the other side. When the toast is crispy on the outside, remove from heat and place on paper towels. Place some powdered sugar into a fine sieve and lightly dust the bread.

How to plate: Spoon ½ cup Strawberry-Peach Compote on bottom of a deep-dish bowl. Unevenly stack three 2-slice "sandwiches" or desired amount of French toast on top of each other. Dust with powdered sugar again and drizzle with maple syrup. Guten Appetit!

Cherry-Walnut Spelt Scones

Makes 8 Scones

❖ ❖ ❖ ❖ ❖ ❖ ❖ ❖ ❖ ❖ ❖ ❖

2 cups spelt flour

1 tablespoon baking powder

1 teaspoon sea salt

⅓ cup canola oil

⅓ cup + ¼ cup (for glazing) agave nectar

¼ cup cold water

1 tablespoon vanilla extract

1 cup dried cherries (soaked in hot water for 15 minutes)

½ cup walnuts, coarsely chopped

These delicious scones are easy to make and a delight to eat. You can use just about any kind of dried or fresh fruit and a variety of different nuts. For example, try blueberries and almonds or cranberries and pecans. These make a delightful light breakfast or snack, delicious with a hot beverage.

Preparation:
Pre-heat oven to 375 degrees F. Line a cookie sheet with parchment paper.

Place flour, baking powder and salt in a bowl and mix. Add oil, ½ cup agave nectar, water and vanilla and mix for about 45 seconds. Gently fold in cherries and walnuts.

Form scones by hand by first dividing dough into 8 parts. Then make each section into a ball. You can form ball into either a square or triangular shape (or whatever your preference) using your hands, then place on cookie sheet. Bake for 8 minutes. Remove from oven and brush with remaining agave nectar, then return to oven for 3 to 4 minutes—until lightly browned.

Allow to cool completely before serving.

Authentic Mexican Tortillas With Guacamole

Makes 6 tortillas

❖ ❖ ❖ ❖ ❖ ❖ ❖ ❖ ❖ ❖ ❖ ❖

1 cup *masa harina*—a flour made from dried corn kernels that have been cooked in limewater (water mixed with calcium oxide)—do not use corn meal.

1 cup warm water (amount varies by brand of *masa harina*)

1 to 2 cloves garlic pressed or finely minced (optional)

1 jalapeño pepper seeded and diced small (optional)

Once you've made homemade tortillas, especially these excellent offerings from Chef Jesús González, store-bought varieties will never be the same. You'll need a tortilla press (available at cooking stores and online); two square sheets cut from a plastic freezer bag (the plastic sheets will be reusable) to fit the press; and an ungreased cast-iron skillet or grill.

Preparation:

In a bowl, mix the *masa harina* and ¾ cup of the water. Add the prepared garlic and jalapeño pepper.

Knead mixture for about 5 minutes. Hint: lightly coat your hands with olive oil to prevent dough from sticking to them. If the dough seems too dry, add more water a little at a time. If the dough is too wet (it will stick to the plastic sheets used when pressing it), add more masa harina a little at a time.

Pinch off golf ball-sized (about 1½-inches) of dough, and roll into balls. Place each ball of dough in a pan or dish and keep covered with a damp cloth to prevent the dough from drying out.

Heat the ungreased frying pan or griddle to medium-high.

If you are using a tortilla press, open the press and put the plastic sheet on the bottom plate. Place one ball of dough on the sheet—slightly off-center toward the hinge of the press. Place the second sheet of plastic on top of the dough. Close and operate the press with moderate pressure.

Re-oil your hands if necessary to prevent dough from sticking, and carefully peel the plastic one side at a time from the flattened dough—ending up with the tortilla laying on one hand. (Reminder: If the dough is sticking to the plastic, it is too wet. Put all the dough back into the mixing bowl and add more *masa harina* a teaspoon at a time and knead until a good consistency is achieved.)

Carefully lay the tortilla flat on the hot skillet or grill. This can take some practice. Start by placing a leading edge down and then trail or drape the remainder.

Cook for about 30 seconds on one side and turn. Cook for about 60 seconds and turn again. Cook for another 30 seconds on the first side. The tortilla will have some brown spots and be slightly puffed when done. Remove the tortilla and keep warm in a basket or dish lined with a cloth that can fold over the top of the tortillas.

Tortillas are best enjoyed while fresh and warm. Leftovers can be wrapped and stored in the refrigerator for 2 to 3 days and reheated. Suggested toppings for the cooked tortillas include guacamole, salsa, refried beans, chopped red onions, and shredded lettuce.

Guacamole

Serves 4

2 avocados, peeled and seeded

1 scallion (mainly whites), finely chopped

½ or less, small red onion, diced

2 cloves minced garlic

1 jalapeño pepper, seeded and minced

1 fresh lime, juiced

½ tomato, diced

2 tablespoons chopped fresh cilantro

Sea salt

Preparation:
Choose an avocado that has give to it. Peel and seed the avocado and mash it with a fork. Transfer the mashed avocado to a bowl and combine with remaining ingredients, including salt to taste. Cover and refrigerate for up to 2 hours.

Tip: A pit left in the guacamole, and a sprinkling of lemon or lime juice, helps to preserve the guacamole's hue of vibrant green. Stir lightly before serving.

Wheat-Free Apple Cinnamon Muffins

Makes 24 muffins

3 medium bananas

2 tablespoons hazelnut oil or other cold pressed oil

12-ounces Silken Tofu

3 tablespoons vanilla extract

½ cup syrup of agave or maple syrup

1 cup organic unfiltered apple juice

1 cup tapioca flour

1 cup corn flour

1 cup brown rice flour

1 tablespoon baking powder

1½ tablespoons baking soda

1 tablespoon ground cinnamon

Thanks to Chef Jesús González at Rancho La Puerta Fitness Resort. These low-fat muffins are dairy, egg and gluten-free. They also happen to be scrumptious.

Preparation:
Pre-heat oven to 350 degrees F.

In a blender or processor, mix the bananas, oil, tofu, vanilla, apple juice and syrup. Purée until smooth.

In a medium bowl, mix all the dry ingredients. Make a well and pour in the liquid mix. Mix until well incorporated.

Pour batter into muffin tins sprayed with no-stick cooking spray. Fill each cup ⅔ full. Bake for 25 to 30 minutes or until the tops are nicely browned and a toothpick comes out clean.

Indulgent Banana Muffins

Makes 12 to 16 muffins

❖ ❖ ❖ ❖ ❖ ❖ ❖ ❖ ❖ ❖ ❖ ❖

4 large, very ripe bananas, mashed

1 cup, less 2 tablespoons, vegan cane sugar

1 tablespoon molasses

1 tablespoon brown rice syrup

½ cup safflower oil

1 tablespoon flax seeds + 3 tablespoons very warm water for flax "eggs"

2 cups whole wheat pastry flour

1 teaspoon aluminum-free baking powder

1 teaspoon baking soda

½ teaspoon fine salt

½ cup finely chopped walnuts

1 cup vegan chocolate chips

2 teaspoons vanilla extract

These decadent muffins, courtesy of Trish Sebben-Krupka, are delicious served warm or at room temperature. While they taste best freshly baked, they will hold for several days well-wrapped, and make a great "grab and go" breakfast or snack.

Flax "Eggs" Preparation:
Place flax seeds and warm water in a small bowl. Soak for 45 minutes to 1 hour. Mixture will be thick and gelatinous. If you don't like whole flax seeds in your muffin, you can purée the mixture in the blender after soaking.

Muffin Preparation:
Place an oven rack in the lower third of the oven; pre-heat oven to 350 degrees F. Line muffin pan(s) with paper liners, or grease lightly.

In a large bowl, mix mashed bananas, sugar, molasses, brown rice syrup, safflower oil and flax eggs.

Whisk flour, baking powder, baking soda and salt in a small bowl. Quickly fold dry ingredients into wet. When nearly combined, fold in walnuts, chocolate chips and vanilla extract. Do not over mix!

Bake for 22 to 25 minutes until muffins are golden brown and slightly springy to the touch.

Cool for 10 minutes in muffin pan on a wire rack before removing them.

Everyone's Favorite Cinnamon Rolls

Makes 12 Rolls

❖ ❖ ❖ ❖ ❖ ❖ ❖ ❖ ❖ ❖ ❖ ❖

ROLLS:

2 ½ teaspoons active dry yeast

½ cup unbleached sugar

1 cup soy milk, warmed

2 tablespoons ground flaxseeds whisked together with 6 tablespoons hot water

⅓ cup vegan margarine, melted

4 ½ cups all-purpose (or spelt) flour

1 teaspoon salt

1 cup brown sugar, packed

2 ½ tablespoons ground cinnamon

ICING

⅓ cup margarine, softened

2 cups Hain Organic Powdered Sugar

1 teaspoon vanilla extract

¼ cup vegan margarine

2 to 4 tablespoons soy milk

Thanks to Evan McGraw from Vancouver, Canada for this decadent recipe. These sticky, gooey buns are worth the work, fat and calories.

Preparation:

Mix yeast, unbleached sugar, and heated soy milk in a large mixing bowl and let stand until foamy. Add flaxseed mixture, melted margarine, flour, and salt. Mix well and knead for 5 to 10 minutes. The dough should be firm and smooth, not sticky. Set the dough aside in a covered bowl for about 1 hour, or until it has doubled in size.

After the dough has doubled, turn it out onto a floured work surface, cover, and let rest for 10 more minutes. Meanwhile, in a small bowl, combine brown sugar and cinnamon.

Roll dough into a 16 x 21-inch rectangle. Spread dough with margarine and sprinkle evenly with sugar/cinnamon mixture. Roll up dough and cut into 12 sections with a sharp knife.

Place rolls on a lightly greased 9x13-inch baking pan. (A cookie sheet also works fine.) Cover and let rise until nearly doubled, about 30 minutes. Meanwhile, pre-heat oven to 400 degrees F. Bake rolls in pre-heated oven until golden brown, about 15 minutes.

While rolls are baking, beat together margarine, powdered sugar, vanilla, and add soy milk 1 tablespoon at a time until desired consistency is reached. Spread frosting on warm rolls before serving.

Sweet Potato Pancakes

Makes about 6 large pancakes

❖ ❖ ❖ ❖ ❖ ❖ ❖ ❖ ❖ ❖ ❖ ❖

1 cup all purpose flour

1 cup whole wheat flour

2 tablespoons sugar

4 tablespoons baking powder

2 cups soy milk

4 tablespoons canola oil

½ cup mashed sweet potatoes

Thanks to Chef Mike Behrend from Green Restaurant in San Antonio, Texas. Sweet potato pancakes can be served with vegan butter and drizzled with warm maple syrup. Crushed pecans and a sprinkle of cinnamon make them even more divine.

Preparation:
Mix all dry ingredients thoroughly in a large mixing bowl. Add soy milk and oil. Stir until combined, but still a little lumpy. Add the mashed sweet potato and fold into the batter.

Ladle the batter into a hot, lightly oiled grill or pan. Pancakes should be about 6-inches in diameter. When bubbles form throughout the pancake, flip it and cook for approximately 2 minutes on the other side.

Whole Wheat Baguettes

Makes 2 loaves or 2 baguettes

❖ ❖ ❖ ❖ ❖ ❖ ❖ ❖ ❖ ❖ ❖

1 cup lukewarm water

¼ teaspoon sugar

2 teaspoons dry packaged yeast, e.g., Fleischmann's (but not "Rapid Rise")

2 cups white bread flour (or substitute all-purpose flour)

¼ cup rye flour

½ cup whole wheat flour

1½ tablespoons wheat germ

3 tablespoons sunflower seeds (optional*)

1½ teaspoons salt

1 tablespoon corn, safflower, or canola oil, plus some for bowl and baking sheet/bread pans

There is nothing like fresh, homemade bread. This easy and delicious recipe from Lee Zucker makes either two crusty baguettes or two loaves of bread. Serve with soup, stew, salad or use for sandwiches. Bread is great with everything.

Preparation:
Combine first three ingredients in a small bowl, stirring. Leave for 5 to 10 minutes, until bubbly. If not bubbly, yeast is dead; do not proceed with recipe. Replace yeast.

Add next 6 ingredients to a large mixing bowl or the work bowl of a standing mixer equipped with a dough hook (made, for example, by KitchenAid). Mix well with a wooden spoon or on low setting if using a machine. When yeast mixture is ready, mix in well. Add oil and mix until totally blended, using your hands as needed. Add a little water if dough is too dry; or some flour if too sticky to pull cleanly away from the sides of the bowl. On a damp day dough may need a little more flour than specified.

Kneading by hand: Turn out onto a lightly floured surface and knead 8 to10 minutes, until smooth and bouncy. Add only enough flour to prevent dough sticking to kneading surface. **Kneading by machine:** Increase speed to medium for several minutes; scrape down and redistribute as needed, adding only enough flour to prevent dough sticking to dough hook. Turn out dough and hand-knead a few times to be sure it is uniformly satiny.

Place kneaded dough in an oiled bowl, turn dough over to grease top also, and cover with a clean non-terry (i.e., fuzz-free), towel that has been dipped in hot water and wrung out well. Put in a warm place (80 to 85 degrees F) to rise until double in bulk—about 1½ hours. (An unheated oven with the light on is ideal.)

When dough has doubled in bulk, punch down, turn out onto a clean, unfloured surface and cut in half.

For baguettes: Flatten each half with lightly floured palms to a rectangle about 3 x 9- inches. (Use a little flour under dough if it sticks to work surface badly.) Roll each loaf up very tightly from the 9-inch side; then roll under your palms firmly, to seal surfaces into a solid tube and extend to about 14-inches long. Dip the bottom of each baguette in a little flour and place on an oiled baking sheet or in a French bread pan.

For loaf bread: Lightly oil 2 loaf pans. After halving dough, tuck raw edges of each loaf underneath itself to make a smooth mound; gently press under your palms until each is roughly loaf shaped. Place in pans.

Cover (either shape) loosely with a clean, dry kitchen towel and leave to rise in a warm place (but not inside the oven) for 45 minutes. Meanwhile, pre-heat oven to 425 degrees F.

Bake on center rack for 20 minutes at 425 degrees F. Reduce temperature to 325 degrees F, rotate pan(s) for even baking, and bake an additional 20 to 25 minutes—until baguettes are nicely tanned and sound hollow when thumped on their undersides. Loaf bread is done when it is tanned on top, shrinks from sides of pan slightly, and/or sounds hollow when carefully tipped out of pan and tapped on the bottom. Remove from pans to rack and cool before slicing.

* Pumpkin seeds, black onion seeds (called nigella or kalunji in Asian and Indian food shops), poppy-seeds, or sesame seeds are all good in this bread instead of or in combination with sunflower seed. Add to taste.

Jumbo Apple Muffins

**Makes 6 jumbo
or giant-sized muffins**

❖ ❖ ❖ ❖ ❖ ❖ ❖ ❖ ❖ ❖ ❖ ❖

2 cups flour

2 teaspoons baking powder

1 teaspoon salt

1 cup Florida Crystals natural sugar

1 teaspoon cinnamon

¾ cup soy milk

½ cup Tofutti brand Imitation Sour Cream

¼ cup canola oil

Ener-G Egg Replacer (mix according to box instructions to make equivalent of 1 egg)

1 cup chopped apples

Look for commercial-quality 6-cup Crown or Giant Muffin Pan where each cup holds about ¾ cups of batter. These breakfast muffins are impressive.

Preparation:
Set oven to 400 degrees F. Spray a 6-cup crown or giant muffin pan with nonstick cooking spray.

In one bowl, mix the dry ingredients. In another bowl, mix the wet ingredients. Then add wet to the dry and stir in chopped apple, using care not to over-mix the batter.

Divide the batter among the cups of the prepared pan. Bake the muffins about 25 minutes, until the mufins are golden and a toothpick inserted into the center comes out clean.

Transfer the pan to a wire rack and let cool for 5 minutes. Unmold the muffins and serve warm or at room temperature.

Desserts

Chocolate Marbled Pound Cake

Photograph: Jane Seymour

Chocolate Marbled Pound Cake

Serves 8

❖ ❖ ❖ ❖ ❖ ❖ ❖ ❖ ❖ ❖ ❖

5 ½ ounces (11 tablespoons) vegan margarine at room temperature, cut in small pieces, plus more to grease pan

2 cups all-purpose flour

1 teaspoon baking soda

1 teaspoon baking powder

½ teaspoon salt

1 cup sugar

1 cup buttermilk replacement (1 cup soy milk plus 2 teaspoons white vinegar)

Ener-G Egg Replacer (mix according to box instructions to make equivalent of 2 eggs)

1 ½ teaspoons vanilla extract

3 tablespoons unsweetened cocoa, sifted

½ cup semisweet chocolate chips

4 ounces bittersweet chocolate, in bits

3 tablespoons light corn syrup

1 teaspoon almond extract

The traditional pound cake recipe is quite popular in Southern United States. As kitchen lore has it, a pound of all the major ingredients would go into the cake. This version is slightly lighter, but in our new version we add enough chocolate for a group of eight to be perfectly satisfied.

Preparation:

Heat oven to 350 degrees F. Grease a 9-by-5-by-3-inch loaf pan with vegan margarine.

Mix flour, baking soda, baking powder and salt together.

Beat 4 ounces margarine in electric mixer until light. Gradually beat in sugar. Increase speed to high, and beat until fluffy. Add egg replacer until just combined.

On low speed, add flour mixture alternately with buttermilk replacement, adding vanilla with the last of it. End with flour mixture.

Transfer ⅔ of batter to greased pan. Add cocoa to remaining batter, mix to blend well, and fold in chocolate chips. Drop chocolate batter over batter in loaf pan, and swirl gently with metal spatula or knife to marbelize. Bake until cake tester comes out clean, about 50 to 55 minutes. Set on rack to cool, then remove from pan.

To make glaze, combine remaining margarine and bittersweet chocolate in double-boiler over very low heat until not quite fully melted. Remove from heat, and stir until chocolate is completely melted. Whisk in corn syrup and almond extract. Set aside until ready to use.

Drizzle glaze over cooled cake, and allow to set about 1 hour before cutting.

Coconut Cake

Serves 8

❖ ❖ ❖ ❖ ❖ ❖ ❖ ❖ ❖ ❖ ❖ ❖

1⅓ cups dried, unsweetened, coconut flakes, plus 1 tablespoon of coconut to coat side of pan

1 cup vegan margarine

1 teaspoon coconut extract or flavoring

1 cup Florida Crystals sugar

¾ cup coconut milk

1½ cups flour

Egg replacer equivalent to 3 eggs

FROSTING

¼ cup (4 tablespoons) vegan margarine

½ of one 8-ounce package of Tofutti "better than Cream Cheese"

½ pound Hain Organic Powdered Sugar

¼ teaspoon vanilla or coconut extract

½ cup shredded coconut

This dense, low-rising, and delicious cake, offered by Claudette Vaughan of the *Abolitionist Online,* is perfect with just about any fresh fruit and icing combination.

Preparation:
Lightly grease a 9-inch round cake pan and sprinkle sides lightly with extra coconut.

Beat margarine, coconut extract, sugar, and coconut milk in large mixing bowl until pale and thick, about 3 to 5 minutes. Fold in the flour and coconut.

Mix egg replacer with water until frothy. Fold into the mixture. Batter will be a bit thick.

Pour into cake pan and spread evenly. Bake at 325 degrees F for about 35 to 40 minutes.

Frosting Preparation:
Leave margarine out in room temperature to soften slightly, and then combine with the refrigerated package of Tofutti "Better than Cream Cheese." Add 1 pound Hain Organic Powdered Sugar, the vanilla or coconut extract, and 1 cup shredded coconut. Combine food processor. Stir in shredded coconut.

Tip: Please refer to the Glossary at the end of this book to find out about Tofutti vegan products.

Kiwi Parfait

Serves 6

❖ ❖ ❖ ❖ ❖ ❖ ❖ ❖ ❖ ❖ ❖ ❖

5 kiwis, peeled and cut into bite-size pieces

1 pint soy yogurt

1 cup crushed graham crackers

CURRIED CASHEWS
  1 cup cashews

  ½ teaspoon canola oil

  ½ teaspoon curry powder

  Salt to taste

Thanks to Chef Cat Cora whose recipe appears in *Great Chefs Cook Vegan* by Linda Long. Parfaits are beautiful, and because they are layered, no bite ever tastes the same.

Preparation:
Place a spoonful of kiwi pieces in the bottom of a martini glass. Top with soy yogurt to cover, and then add a layer of graham crackers. Notice how the layers are shaping from the outside of the glass. Repeat layers of kiwi and yogurt. Top with Curried Cashews and a few kiwi pieces.

To make the Curried Cashews: Pre-heat oven to 350 degrees F. Place cashews on an unlined baking sheet and bake for 12 minutes, or until fragrant and slightly browned. Toss nuts with canola oil and curry powder in a bowl. Add salt, if desired, and then cool.

Two-Layer Thanksgiving Cheesecake

Serves 8 to 10

❖ ❖ ❖ ❖ ❖ ❖ ❖ ❖ ❖ ❖ ❖ ❖

BOTTOM LAYER

½ package Mori-Nu Lite Firm Tofu

4 ounces Tofutti "Better Than Cream Cheese"

½ cup canned pumpkin

½ cup Florida Crystals natural sugar

1½ tablespoons flour

¾ teaspoon cinnamon

¼ teaspoon powdered ginger

¼ teaspoon ground nutmeg

1 tablespoon pure molasses

⅛ teaspoon baking soda

Small pinch of salt

TOP LAYER

1 cup pumpkin

½ cup sunflower seed butter

1½ teaspoons ground ginger

1 teaspoon cinnamon

¼ teaspoon ground nutmeg

1 cup sugar

Ener-G Egg Replacer (Mix according to box instructions to make equivalent of 2 eggs)

Our gratitude for the Two-Layer Thanksgiving Cheesecake goes to Susan Wu, who co-founded the delightful vegan café SuTao in Malvern, Pennsylvania. Susan is a long-time practitioner of Yan Xin Qigong, which focuses on exercises to cultivate vital energy and contributions to the community. That dedication is evident in the restaurant. On occasions special to Chinese culture, and North American holidays too, Susan hosts special buffets to celebrate. In the Delaware Valley, no vegan need ever wonder where to find a festive meal on any holiday.

Lee Hall, co-author of *Dining With Friends: The Art of North American Vegan Cuisine,* says, "Any time I've felt a little under the weather—a headache or soreness in the joints, for example—I go over to SuTao and ask Susan to recommend a meal. I order what Susan recommends, and have always felt back to 100% in forty-eight hours or less."

This smooth cheesecake, attractively layered and not too sweet, is something to be thankful for. But that doesn't mean you have to wait until Thanksgiving to make it.

Preparation of Bottom Layer:
Purée the bottom layer ingredients. Pour into a prepared vegan pie crust such as Arrowhead Mills Graham Cracker Pie Crust. Proceed with top layer.

Preparation of Top Layer:
Using hand mixer, blend all of the top layer ingredients together. Pour on top of the cheesecake batter. Bake at 350 degrees F for 50 minutes. Let cool for 30 minutes then refrigerate 5 to 6 hours or overnight before serving.

Berry, Cherry and Peach Compote

Serves 4

❖ ❖ ❖ ❖ ❖ ❖ ❖ ❖ ❖ ❖ ❖

2 cups fresh raspberries

2 cups blueberries

½ pound large Bing cherries, Halved and pitted

4 peaches, peeled and sliced

¼ cup Florida Crystals sugar

Remember the expression, "the best things in life are free"? Well, really, the best things are blueberries, cherries and peaches. They aren't always free, but they are always delectable.

Preparation:
Toss blueberries, cherries and peaches with sugar. Place fruit in clean bowl and sprinkle with raspberries. Serve plain or with sorbet.

Fresh Blueberry Tart

Serves 6 to 8

❖ ❖ ❖ ❖ ❖ ❖ ❖ ❖ ❖ ❖ ❖

CRUST

1¼ cups graham cracker crumbs

¼ cup Florida Crystals sugar

⅓ cup melted vegan margarine

FILLING

1 quart blueberries, washed, drained and hulled

⅔ cup water

1 cup Florida Crystals sugar

3 tablespoons cornstarch

⅓ cup cold water

Blueberries are often described as a "superfood." But what's so super about blueberries? They are perfect in just about anything. You won't be able to resist this fruity tart.

Preparation for crust:
Combine graham cracker crumbs, sugar and melted vegan margarine. Press mixture 1-inch up the sides and over the bottom of a 9-inch springform pan. Bake at 375 degrees F for 6 to 8 minutes until golden. Let crust cool before adding blueberry mixture.

Preparation for filling:
Place 1 cup of blueberries and ⅔ cup water in a 2 quart pan and simmer for about 3 minutes. Blend together sugar, cornstarch and cold water and add to the simmering mixture. Boil for 2 minutes, stirring constantly. Turn heat off and add remaining 3 cups blueberries.

When the blueberry mixture is lukewarm, pour it into the graham cracker crust. Refrigerate tart in springform pan until ready to serve.

Berry Parfait With Avocado Cream

Serves 6

❖ ❖ ❖ ❖ ❖ ❖ ❖ ❖ ❖ ❖ ❖ ❖

1 medium ripe avocado (about 7.5–8.5 ounces)

½ cup extra firm silken tofu

1 cup organic vanilla soy milk

2 tablespoons brandy

2 tablespoons fructose

1 tablespoon pure vanilla extract

Zest from 1 orange

1 ½ cups blueberries (6 ounces)

1 ½ cups sliced strawberries or raspberries

6 whole strawberries for garnish

Recipe created by Chef Jesús González of La Cocina Que Canta Culinary Center at Rancho La Puerta Fitness Resort & Spa. Yes, fresh berries taste great all by themselves. But this sauce, which only takes a few minutes to prepare, makes fresh, seasonal fruit sing.

Preparation:

To make the avocado cream, in a blender cup or processor bowl combine the avocado, tofu, soy milk, brandy, fructose, vanilla and zest. Process until smooth and creamy.

Place ½ cup berries in 6 champagne glasses or dessert cups. Top with 2 ounces of the avocado cream and garnish with a fanned strawberry. To fan the strawberry, cut thin slices from tip up to but not through the stem end. Fan slice out.

Raspberry Pie

Serves 6–8

❖ ❖ ❖ ❖ ❖ ❖ ❖ ❖ ❖ ❖ ❖

4 cups fresh raspberries

1 cup Florida Crystals sugar

½ cup water

2 heaping tablespoons cornstarch

One 9-inch baked pie shell

Non-dairy whipped topping or soy ice cream

Apples aren't the only pie-worthy fruit. Raspberries make a delightfully tart, but sweet pie. Of course you should scoop some ice cream onto this while it's still slightly warm.

Preparation:
Set 3 cups of raspberries aside. Combine remaining cup with sugar, water, and cornstarch in a medium-sized pot. Cook over low heat until the mixture thickens. Put the remaining 3 cups of cold raspberries in the pie shell. Add the thickened raspberry concoction and turn over a few times. Chill for 1 hour. Serve with non-dairy whipped topping or soy ice cream.

Chocolate Pudding With Berries

Serves 3 to 4

❖ ❖ ❖ ❖ ❖ ❖ ❖ ❖ ❖ ❖ ❖

1½ cups fresh berries (blackberries, raspberries or blueberries)

5 ounces organic bittersweet dark chocolate

3 tablespoons Florida Crystals sugar

¼ cup water

6 ounces firm silken tofu

Calling that instant stuff that comes in a box "pudding" is an insult to puddings everywhere. Why bother with a box when this luscious, creamy pudding is almost as fast and just as easy?

Preparation:
Melt sugar and chocolate in double boiler.

Place tofu, water and chocolate in a food processor and blend until smooth, about 2 minutes. Place pudding in parfait glasses, refrigerate for at least 2 hours and top with berries.

Variation: Several pieces of candied ginger blended into the pudding makes a wonderful addition.

Mango Tango Flan

Serves 8 to 10

❖ ❖ ❖ ❖ ❖ ❖ ❖ ❖ ❖ ❖ ❖ ❖ ❖

CRUST

1 cup finely ground walnuts

⅓ cup finely ground rolled oats

1 tablespoon corn starch or arrowroot

¼ teaspoon cinnamon

½ cup spelt flour

¼ cup maple syrup

2 tablespoons brown rice syrup

1 teaspoon vanilla

1 tablespoon canola oil

FILLING

1 cup pineapple juice

¾ cup water

1 ripe mango, peeled and diced (about 1 cup)

2 tablespoons agar-agar flakes (or 1 ½ teaspoons agar powder)

One 12-ounce package firm silken tofu (Mori Nu)

½ cup maple syrup

1 ½ teaspoons vanilla

¼ teaspoon salt

½ teaspoon turmeric

GLAZE

3 tablespoons apricot preserves

2 tablespoons water

Submitted by vegan personal chef Mary Lawrence of Connecticut. More tangy than sweet, this dessert is as pretty as it is delicious. If you can't imagine using tofu in a dessert, go ahead and try it. You're in for a delicious surprise.

Preparation of crust:
In a food processor, pulse walnuts and oats until they are finely ground. Add remaining dry ingredients and pulse together with maple syrup, rice syrup, vanilla and oil until a batter forms. The batter may be a little sticky (and this is normal). With an oiled spatula, spread batter into a greased 8-inch springform pan. Bake at 350 degrees F for 12 to 15 minutes, or until lightly browned. Set aside to cool.

Preparation of filling:
In a small pot, boil mango, juice and water on medium high heat for about 1 minute. Remove from heat and set mango aside in a blender. Return pot of juice to burner and dissolve agar agar in it. Bring to a slow boil over medium heat then simmer for approximately 5 minutes, until it begins to thicken. Pour liquid into blender with mango, banana, tofu, syrup, vanilla, salt and turmeric. Purée until smooth (you may need to do this in two batches). Pour filling into cooled shell and refrigerate for several hours before serving.

Preparation of glaze:
Heat preserves and water in a small saucepan until it becomes a liquid. Bring to a boil for about a minute until it thickens. Once filling has set, pour glaze over the top and garnish with "half moon" slices of lime.

Mignardises (Chocolate Truffles)

Yields about 80 half-teaspoon pieces

❖ ❖ ❖ ❖ ❖ ❖ ❖ ❖ ❖ ❖

1 cup raw cashew butter

1 cup maple syrup

1 cup cocoa powder.

½ teaspoon vanilla seeds, scraped from a vanilla bean that's split lengthwise

1 tablespoon nama shoyu (raw soy sauce)

Variety of coatings such as coconut, sesame seeds, crushed pumpkin seeds, cayenne pepper, or chopped dried fruit.

Thanks to Chefs Charlie Trotter and Matthias Merges whose recipe appears in *Great Chefs Cook Vegan* by Linda Long. These gorgeous truffles make great gifts, but please be sure to save some (OK—a lot) for yourself.

Preparation:
Combine well in a food processor. Pour into a shallow container, cover, refrigerate 4 hours. With a melon baller, scrape chocolate truffle mix into small balls. Fill or roll pieces with cocoa, spices, cayenne pepper, mint, nuts, seeds, sugars, dried fruit or zests, shaping as desired.

Photograph: Linda Long

Orange-Poppy Seed Cake

Serves 12 to 15

❖ ❖ ❖ ❖ ❖ ❖ ❖ ❖ ❖ ❖ ❖ ❖ ❖

CAKE
4 ½ cups plain flour

⅓ cup poppy seeds

3 teaspoons cinnamon

1 tablespoon baking powder

1 teaspoon baking soda

1 cup light brown sugar

1 cup apple juice

1 cup orange juice

½ cup water

¾ safflower oil

ORANGE GLAZE
1 cup Hain Organic Powered Sugar

1 tablespoon orange juice

1 tablespoon rice milk

¼ teaspoon orange extract

This recipe comes courtesy of Claudette Vaughan, editor of *Abolitionist Online.*

Preparation:
Mix all dry ingredients together. Mix all wet ingredients together. Fold gently together. Pour into greased Bundt cake pan.

Bake in pre-heated oven 350 degrees F for 40 minutes or until toothpick comes out clean. Cook cake in pan for 10 minutes, and then turn onto wire rack to finish cooking. Cool cake completely before glazing.

Raspberry-Apple Crumble

Serves 4

❖ ❖ ❖ ❖ ❖ ❖ ❖ ❖ ❖ ❖ ❖

2 cups fresh raspberries

3 Granny Smith apples, peeled, seeded and sliced

1 cup flour

½ cup Florida Crystals sugar

½ cup soy margarine

¼ teaspoon nutmeg

Fresh lemon juice from 1 lemon

When it's cold outside, there's something therapeutic and invigorating about a fresh fruit crumble.

Preparation:
Pre-heat oven to 375 degrees F. Peel and core apples and slice each into 8 to 10 pieces. Arrange in baking dish, sprayed with vegetable oil. Squeeze lemon juice over them.

Drain the raspberries and sprinkle them over the apples.

Mix flour and sugar in a bowl. Cut in the margarine with a knife until the mixture is crumbly. Add nutmeg and cover fruit with this mixture.

Bake for about 25 minutes until the top is golden brown.

Serve accompanied with vanilla non-dairy ice cream.

Ice Cream and Sorbet

Blueberry-Pomegranate Sorbet

Photograph: Jane Seymour

Blueberry-Pomegranate Sorbet

Photograph: Jane Seymour

Makes about 4 cups

❖ ❖ ❖ ❖ ❖ ❖ ❖ ❖ ❖ ❖ ❖

1 ¼ cup sugar syrup (see below)

¼ cup unsweetened Pomegranate juice

4 cups fresh blueberries

1 tablespoon lemon juice

1 ½ teaspoons each grated lemon and lime zest

Option: Garnish with mint leaves and pomegranate seeds

This gorgeous sorbet is high in antioxidants. When your guests think they're full, wait until they've had one spoonful of this striking dessert. Before you know it, they'll be asking for a second serving. Try it and see.

Preparation:

To make sugar syrup, combine 1¼ cups Florida Crystals sugar with 1¼ cups water in saucepan. Bring to a boil and cook until sugar is dissolved, stirring occasionally. Set aside and cool to room temperature or refrigerate.

Purée the blueberries with the sugar syrup, lemon juice, zest and Pomegranate juice in a blender until very smooth. Strain through a fine-mesh strainer for smooth texture.

Cover and refrigerate until cool; then churn in an ice cream maker according to the manufacturer's directions.

Cantaloupe Sorbet

Makes about 4 cups

❖ ❖ ❖ ❖ ❖ ❖ ❖ ❖ ❖ ❖ ❖

1 cup sugar syrup*

4 cups seeded, cubed and peeled cantaloupe

¼ cup fresh squeezed orange juice

1½ teaspoons grated lemon zest

Option: 2 tablespoons vodka

Sorbet is a refreshing respite from the summer heat. Here, melon and citrus combine to form a pleasing and tangy frozen treat.

Preparation:
*To make sugar syrup, combine 1 cup Florida Crystals sugar with 1 cup water in saucepan. Bring to a boil and cook until sugar is dissolved, stirring occasionally. Set aside and cool to room temperature or refrigerate.

Purée the cantaloupe, sugar syrup, lemon zest and vodka in a blender until very smooth.

Cover and refrigerate until cool; then churn in an ice cream maker according to the manufacturer's directions. Freeze about 2 hours or until firm before serving.

Note: Vodka (or any other type of alcohol) helps produce a soft sorbet. Alcohol doesn't freeze and adding a small amount keeps the sorbet from getting icy. Vodka doesn't affect the taste.

Peanut Butter-Coconut Ice Cream

Serves 6

❖ ❖ ❖ ❖ ❖ ❖ ❖ ❖ ❖ ❖

One 13.5-ounce can light coconut milk (1½ cups)

½ cup maple syrup

½ cup crunchy peanut butter

1 teaspoon vanilla extract

1 cup French Vanilla soy creamer

Reprinted with permission of *Vegetarian Times,* here's the ultimate ice cream recipe: creamy, luscious, nutty and a hint of coconut. Perfection.

Preparation:
Purée coconut milk, maple syrup, peanut butter, vanilla extract and soy creamer in blender until smooth.

Chill and refrigerate until cool; then process in an ice cream maker according to the manufacturer's directions.

Peach Ice Cream

Makes about 4 cups

❖ ❖ ❖ ❖ ❖ ❖ ❖ ❖ ❖ ❖ ❖

2 cups fresh peaches, peeled

½ peach, peeled and cut up held in reserve

6 ounces silken firm tofu, drained

½ cup light coconut milk

½ cup agave nectar or ¾ cup sugar syrup

2 teaspoons pure vanilla extract

1 tablespoon lemon zest

No one can resist ripe, juicy, summer peaches—especially when they come together in ice cream. This dish as enjoyable to make as it is to eat.

Preparation:
If using sugar syrup instead of agave nectar, combine ¾ cup Florida Crystals sugar with ¾ cup water in saucepan. Bring to a boil and cook until syrup is dissolved, stirring occasionally. Set aside and cool to room temperature or refrigerate.

Purée peeled peaches and tofu in blender until smooth. Add coconut milk, agave nectar, vanilla extract and lemon zest. Purée until smooth.

Process in an ice cream maker according to manufacturer's directions.

During last 5 minutes of processing in ice cream maker, quickly peel and chop ½ peach and add to ice cream maker while paddles are still going. Serve or transfer to container to freeze.

Raspberry-Banana Smoothie

Serves 4

❖ ❖ ❖ ❖ ❖ ❖ ❖ ❖ ❖ ❖ ❖

4 cups raspberries

2 bananas

1 cup orange juice

3 tablespoons fresh lime juice

½ cup crushed ice

Mint leaves for garnish

A smoothie is a refreshing and healthful choice for any time of day, any day of the year.

Preparation:
In a blender, combine the ingredients and process until smooth. Pour into glasses and garnish with mint.

Watermelon Sorbet

Makes about 4 cups

❖ ❖ ❖ ❖ ❖ ❖ ❖ ❖ ❖ ❖ ❖

1 cup sugar syrup (see below)

4 cups seeded, chopped watermelon

¼ cup lime juice

½ teaspoon grated lime zest

1 to 2 tablespoons vodka

Often, store-bought sorbet tastes more like sugar than the ingredient for which it is inspired: fresh fruit. Juicy watermelon makes this sorbet light and refreshing. The perfect ending to a hot summer's day.

Preparation:
To make sugar syrup, combine 1 cup Florida Crystals sugar with 1 cup water in saucepan. Bring to a boil and cook until sugar is dissolved, stirring occasionally. Set aside and cool to room temperature or refrigerate.

Purée the watermelon, sugar syrup, lime juice, zest and vodka in a blender until very smooth.

Cover and refrigerate until cool; then churn in an ice cream maker according to the manufacturer's directions.

Note: Vodka (or any other type of alcohol) produces a soft sorbet. Alcohol doesn't freeze and adding a small amount keeps the sorbet from getting icy. Vodka doesn't affect the taste.

Vanilla Mint Chocolate Chip Ice Cream

Makes about 4 cups

❖ ❖ ❖ ❖ ❖ ❖ ❖ ❖ ❖ ❖ ❖

2 cups French Vanilla soy creamer

½ cup agave nectar

1 teaspoon pure peppermint extract

2 tablespoons cornstarch

1 cup light coconut milk

½ cup sweet or bittersweet dark chocolate bar, chopped into very small uneven pieces

With a hint of mint and rich chocolate, and a perfect, creamy texture, this is the perfect summertime treat. And if you don't own an ice cream maker, you might want to consider it. The store-bought versions don't compare.

Preparation:

Put the soy creamer in a saucepan over medium-high heat, stirring and bring just to a boil.

Mix cornstarch with 2 tablespoons of cold water and whisk until smooth.

Add the cornstarch mixture and agave syrup to the soy creamer, whisking constantly over medium heat until slightly thick, about 4 minutes. Add peppermint extract and stir in coconut milk.

Cool about 2 hours and process in an ice cream machine, adding chocolate bits during last 5 minutes while paddles are still going. Transfer to container and freeze.

Glossary

Key to Ingredients, Nutrients, and Vegetarian Terms

Agar-Agar: Agar is a translucent, plant-based nutritive sweetener, derived from red algae. Chiefly from eastern Asia, it is also known as Kanten, Agar-Agar, or Agal-Agal (Ceylon Agar). Most types of agar are purchased in powder form. Dissolved in hot (usually boiling) water and cooled, agar becomes gelatinous, and has featured in traditional Japanese desserts popular for many centuries.

Agave nectar: A sweetener with a consistency similar to honey, agave nectar is suitable for tea or for baking, and provides the natural minerals iron, calcium, potassium, and magnesium. It is extracted from the pineapple-shaped core of the agave, a cactus-like, Central American plant. When baking, a general rule is to replace 1 cup sugar with ¾ cup of agave nectar, and reduce traditional recipe liquids (outside of this book) by ⅓ and oven temperature 25 degrees F. Vegans avoid honey because bees, who are sensitive animals, rely on the honey they create as their sole source of nutrition in cold weather and other times when alternative food sources are not available. In the process of honey collection, some bees are likely to be killed or injured. Apiculture entails the buying and selling of bees, genetic selection techniques, and artificial insemination.

Al dente: Cooked only until tender but still giving some resistance to the bite. Pasta cooked al dente is slightly firm, not soggy or starchy.

Antioxidants: Chemicals thought to protect cells against environmental smog and other possible carcinogens. Steaming vegetables rather than boiling them is best for retaining antioxidants. Research in the *Journal of the Science of Food and Agriculture* indicates that steamed broccoli, for example, lost 11% or fewer of its three major antioxidants. Microwaving seems especially harsh on antioxidants: microwaved broccoli lost between 97% and 74% of the three compounds; in contrast, one antioxidant was not removed at all during steaming. Dr. Cristina Garcia-Viguera, from the University of Porto in Portugal, explains that "most of the bioactive compounds are water soluble; during heating they leach in a high percentage to the cooking water, reducing their nutritional benefits in the foodstuff." That's one reason more antioxidants would be lost upon boiling rather than steaming.

Asafetida Powder: A pungent spice sometimes used in Indian cooking . The spice has a strong garlic smell, but when used delivers a flavor that is similar to leeks. Should be available in a well-stocked bulk section at a co-op or health food store. If unable to locate, substitute using garlic or onion powder—or a combination of both.

Baking powder: Rumsford brand, sold in a red container, works well, and is a safe choice because it does not contain aluminum sulfate (also called aluminum salt). Baking powder stays fresh for about one year.

Brown rice syrup: Brown rice syrup is a naturally processed sweetener, made from sprouted brown rice. It is thick in consistency, and mild in taste.

Blanch: To partially cook by placing the vegetable in cold water, bringing it to a boil, then draining it well and refreshing it in cold water to stop the cooking process.

Bundt cake: Pronounced: bunt (as in "cut") or boont (as in "took"). A ring-shaped cake baked in a tube pan that has fluted sides. Originally a trademark. Source: The American Heritage® Dictionary of the English Language (Fourth Edition, 2000).

Bulgur wheat: Golden beige grain with an irregular, cracked shape. Best known as the main ingredient in tabouli, its higher nutritional value makes it a good substitute for rice or cous cous.

Butter substitutes: See *vegan margarine.*

Calcium stearate: Additive sometimes found in sweets; usually derived from the fat of other animals.

Canola oil: Also known as rapeseed oil, Canola is a versatile cooking oil that is very low in saturated fat and high in monounsaturated fat. It is recognized as a heart-healthy oil by numerous health-professional organizations. Look for organic to avoid the genetically modified variety. Spectrum Organics produces an organic oil that should be widely available. Ideal for sautéing at medium-high heat or, because of its neutral flavor, for baking.

Casein: See *cheese.*

Celery root: Known as "turnip-rooted celery" or "knob celery," celery root is a kind of celery, grown as a root vegetable for its large and well-developed taproot rather than for its stem and leaves. May be used raw or cooked. Celery root has a celery essence, and is often used as a flavoring in soups and stews; it can also be used on its own, usually mashed, or used in casseroles, gratins and baked dishes.

Chocolate: Bittersweet (in 3-ounce bar) Pure Dark Chocolate by *Chocolate Decadence* works well in cheesecake and many other recipes. *Chocolate Decadence* is vegan-owned and -operated. See *www.chocolatedecadence.com* and *http://store.yahoo.com/chocdec/ bittersweet.html.* Both *Ecco Bella* and *Paul Newman's* brands offer vegan chocolate for cooking or indulging, avoiding chocolate made by enslaved workers. An investigation, published in 2000 by the British Broadcasting Company (BBC), reported that hundreds of thousands of children have been purchased from their parents in Mali, Burkina Faso, and Togo for a nominal price and then shipped to the Ivory Coast, where they are sold as slaves to cocoa farms. These children work 80 to 100 hours a week, and are often viciously beaten if they try to escape. Given these circumstances, we think you'll agree that the extra money you pay for fair-trade chocolate is reasonable. For more information on Newman's Own Organics (some of them are vegan) See *www. newmansownorganics.com/food_newman-os.html#.* Green & Blacks Organic Unsweetened Cocoa for baking is fair-trade certified *www.greenandblacks.com.*

Cheese: Vegans avoid cheese and products containing whey (liquid part of animal milk) or caseinates (which contain casein, a protein derived from cow's milk). Although most cheese alternatives state that they do not contain lactose, a dairy-derived sugar, closer reading of the ingredient label reveals that they contain casein. This protein is added to give melted soy cheeses the rubbery texture found in cheese made from the milk of nonhuman animals.

Chocolate chips: See *Tropical Source.*

Chop: To cut into coarse chunks of the size typically found in canned soups.

Cholesterol: Our cells contain cholesterol, naturally produced by the liver. The body needs no additional cholesterol. When cholesterol and fats move through the body, in clusters called lipoproteins, the "Low-density lipoproteins" (LDLs) leave deposits along the walls of the arteries as they travel to the organs. Eventually this process narrows the arteries and obstructs blood flow. Known as hardening of the arteries, this condition is fairly common; but in advanced cases it can leads to heart disease or strokes. Given that LDLs promote atherosclerosis, they are known as "bad cholesterol."

"Good cholesterol," found in "high-density lipoproteins" (HDLs), moves back to the liver where it is cleansed. But most cholesterol is in the form of LDLs, and a high blood cholesterol level means high LDL levels. According to a study published in the *Journal of Chronic Disease* (1978), population groups with cholesterol levels of 150 or less are largely free of atherosclerosis. For cholesterol levels above 150, the risk of heart disease increases.

Saturated fats raise your body's natural cholesterol levels, but added cholesterol is found only in animal products, including shellfish. Basing one's diet on plant foods is the best way to keep saturated fat intake low and to avoid cholesterol. A non-smoking vegan's diet has the lowest risk of heart disease, according to nutritional studies. Research also shows that people who eat small meals frequently throughout the day ("nibblers") have lower cholesterol levels than people who fill up at set meal times ("gorgers"). Additionally, exercise and the use of relaxation techniques such as yoga or meditation help. Combined with a low-fat, pure vegetarian diet, they lower one's cholesterol levels and—according to studies published by Dean Ornish—can even reverse heart disease for many people.

Complementary proteins: See *protein.*

Cremini mushrooms: One of the most widely cultivated mushrooms in the world. This variety of mushroom is actually a small, immature portabella mushroom. They are closely related to the common white mushroom, but considered more flavorful. Also contains high amounts of B-vitamins. Available in most supermarkets.

Dice: To chop finely into tiny cubes.

Egg replacers (Ener-G Egg Replacer): A vegan egg substitute comprised of potato starch, tapioca flour, leavening (non-dairy calcium lactate, calcium carbonate, citric acid), and carbohydrate gum. A 16-ounce box makes the equivalent of 100 eggs. For example, for the equivalent of one egg, mix 2 teaspoons of egg replacer (Ener-G brand) with 2 tablespoon of water and beat with a fork until frothy. To substitute for 2 eggs, mix 4 teaspoons dry Ener-G brand with 4 tablespoons water and beat until frothy.

Another egg substitute is mixing 1 tablespoon flax seeds with 3 tablespoons warm water and allow the mixture to sit until thick (see "Indulgent Banana Muffins" in this book). Or you can use ½ mashed banana; some chefs experiment using avocados.

Why an egg-free cookbook? The intensive egg industry, which began by storing thousands of birds in unused military sheds, is widely considered a model for today's intensive animal agriculture. Some people argue that free-range eggs are acceptable, but most free-range eggs come from birds who are also confined, and are eventually killed; male chicks are often deemed disposable. Moreover, the entire human community cannot afford to have and eat free-range domestic animals. So from a practical standpoint alone, the best idea would be for humanity to design and enjoy a rich variety of plant-based culinary approaches. This is our contribution to that adventure.

Ergocalciferol: See *Vitamin D.*

Fenugreek seed: Fenugreek, frequently used in curry, is used as both an herb (the leaves) and as a spice (the seed). It is featured in cuisines all over the world including Ethiopian, Indian, Eritrean, Turkish, Egyptian, Chinese and many others. By itself, it has a bitter taste and strong smell.

Fish(es): See *pesco-vegetarian.*

Flax seed oil: Omega-3 fatty acids can be boosted by a teaspoon of flax seed oil per day.

Like *kelp* and *Brazil nuts,* flax seed oil has highly concentrated nutrients; don't overdo them. Stick with the product's suggested amount. See also *linolenic acid.*

Florida Crystals sugar: There is no animal bone char or any other animal by product used in the manufacturing of Florida Crystals, a natural sugar produced by the Florida Crystals Corporation of West Palm Beach, Florida. No additives, preservatives, or artificial ingredients are added. Internet ordering is possible, through *http://www. floridacrystals.com/.* The customer service hotline is 877.835.2828.

Fruitarian: One who eats foods that ripen and release naturally, so that harvesting does not kill the plant. A fruitarian will eat apples, but not potatoes.

Garam masala: A basic blend of ground spices to be used alone or with other seasonings. It is common in the Indian, Bangladeshi and Pakistani cuisines. The mixture typically includes cloves, green and/or black/brown cardamom, cinnamon (or probably cassia), and mace and/or nutmeg. Commercially prepared varieties are commonly available at most supermarkets.

Gelatin (also gelatine): A protein product, manufactured by partial hydrolysis of collagen found in animal bones, hooves, connective tissues, and skins. When added to recipes, it produces a gel, commonly found in marshmallows, mints and clear sweets, and also in pharmaceutical capsules. A similar product known as agar (or "agar agar") can be obtained from vegetable sources. Most "kosher gelatin" isn't vegetarian, but Emes kosher gelatin is made from carrageenan (seaweed-based). Guar gum is vegan.

Genetically modified organisms ("GMO"); genetic engineering ("GE"): Although these concepts have been heralded by some politicians as a scientific breakthrough to solve world hunger, the reality is something which we should study closely. Opposition to genetic engineering is not "anti-science" but is a critique of products provided through a specific application of scientific personnel and a decision to allocate resources in a way which is tied to the profits of large companies.

Grapeseed oil: A versatile, flavorless cooking oil used for salad dressings, marinades, deep frying, flavored oils and baking. Because it has a high smoke point, grapeseed oil can withstand hotter cooking temperatures than olive oil. Additionally, grapeseed oil is thought to lower bad cholesterol.

Green mango: The tropical equivalent of a green apple—tart, crisp and somewhat dry.

Hain organic sugars: These include powdered and brown sugar preferred by many vegans. No bone ash is used in the refining process. The powdered version contains organic evaporated cane juice and organic cornstarch; the brown version contains organic evaporated cane juice. Widely available throughout North America.

Herbamare Seasoning: A flavorful blend of sea salt and 14 organic herbs that goes great in place of regular salt on foods.

Herbs: When using fresh herbs, you must use more than you would of the dry version. As a rule, plan a 3-to-1 ratio. For example, if a recipe suggests 1 teaspoon dry dill, you can use 1 tablespoon fresh dill. (A tablespoon is three teaspoons.)

Honey: See *agave nectar.*

Iodine: Nutrient provided by iodized salt or kelp (about 15 grams over the course of a year, or two kelp tablets a week, is about right), or even coconut. Good levels of iodine help maintain a healthy thyroid, and promote high energy, clear skin, and healthy cholesterol levels.

Iron: Dark green, leafy vegetables and beans are a better source of iron than hamburger or milk. Blackstrap molasses, tofu, prune juice, bulgur wheat, dried apricots, raisins, cashews, and dried figs are also excellent sources of iron. Iron deficiency rates are no higher in vegetarians than in the general population. According to the American Dietetic Association, the higher vitamin C content of vegetarian diets may improve iron absorption.

Linolenic acid: The American Dietetic Association recommends that vegetarians include good sources of linolenic acid in their diets. Good sources include flax seed oil, walnuts, and canola oil.

Magnesium: Found in green, leafy vegetables; whole-grain breads, and nuts, magnesium promotes strong bones, a healthy heart and a smoothly functioning nervous system.

Mandoline: A kitchen utensil used to cut hard vegetables and fruits into long, thin strips (juliennes). The utensil is capable of producing varying widths and thicknesses. It also makes slices, waffle cuts and crinkle cuts. Available at kitchen supply stores.

Margarine: See *vegan margarine.*

Masa Harina: Masa harina is a type of traditional flour used in Mexican cooking. Do not substitute corn meal or regular corn flour, however; they're produced from different types of corn and are processed differently. They will not produce the same results. Regular wheat flour also cannot be substituted.

Mince: To chop finely, nearly into a blend (such as minced garlic).

Miso: A paste, either rich dark brown (with a strong taste) or sandy in hue (known as white miso, with a relatively sweet taste), made from soybeans, barley, rice, or a combination of these. Miso is used in spreads, gravies, or as a soup stock. Miso is normally vegan, although some Japanese brands of miso contain a fish extract. Westbrae Natural offers mellow white miso from cultured white rice, organically grown whole soybeans, water, and sea salt.

Nama Shoyu: Advertised as "The Champagne of Soy Sauces," Nama Shoyu is a raw, organic, and unpasteurized soy sauce, similar to miso tamari. It is manufactured by Ohsawa, and has become their best-selling product. Note: Nama Shoyu contains wheat.

Nutritional yeast: Adds taste and a texture slightly reminiscent of cheese. Red Star Vegetarian Support Formula provides B-complex vitamins including a naturally fermented, non-animal source of vitamin B-12.

Olive oil: Extra virgin olive oil is preferred. Has a variety of uses including low-heat cooking and sautéing, use in dressings and cold sauces.

Organics: Products that support sustainable farming, farm worker health, and ecologically-sound processing methods. An official definition adopted by the National Organic Standards Board in 1995 states: "Organic agriculture is an ecological production management system that promotes and enhances biodiversity, biological cycles and soil biological activity. It is based on minimal use of off-farm inputs and on management practices that restore, maintain and enhance ecological harmony." 60 percent of herbicides, 90 percent of fungicides, and 30 percent of insecticides are considered carcinogenic by the U.S. Environmental Protection Agency. The search for alternatives steers consumers to organic products. Now here's the rub: Animal-derived products are often used as fertilizers. Green fertilizers such as seaweed and clover; some gardeners are exploring the use of such products in a practice known as "veganic" gardening. Although organic production on its own guarantees neither a stable livelihood nor long-term environmental sustainability, it undoubtedly takes an important step in the right direction.

Ovo-lacto vegetarian: Person who eats food from vegetable sources, but the prefix "ovo" signifies one who also eats eggs, and the prefix "lacto" signifies one who ingests animal milk products.

Pareve (parve): A kosher classification; made without animal flesh or milk but can contain eggs or fish derivatives.

Pesco-vegetarian: Person who eats a vegetable-based diet but includes marine animal flesh. The idea that marine animals can be compatible with vegetarianism is probably based on the idea that fish swim freely until they get caught, and they don't feel anything when they do. But now that fishing industries have pillaged the open waters, a substantial portion of marketed marine animals grow up in enclosed ponds, or fish farms. And for many years, scientific reports have indicated that fish are sentient and show the same responses we show when we suffer. For instance, a 2003 article in the journal *Nature* indicates that fish feel pain when impaled on hooks. Fish constantly depend on the delicate sensitivity of their mouths to find food. The idea that fish are not conscious seems a throwback to the time of Descartes, the French philosopher who believed that animals feel no pain, and only struggle to escape, yelp, or cry as a mechanical response.

Contrary to some company's claims, fish oil supplements do not lower cholesterol levels in the blood, according to a study published in the *Journal of Lipid Research* by S.M. Grundy and M.A. Denke (1990). A diet including fish is not as beneficial as a pure vegetarian diet.

Potato ricer: Utensil used to process food by forcing it through small holes, which are often not much larger than a grain of rice. Mashed potatoes are a food commonly made using this utensil. In technical terms, it works by a process of extrusion. A potato ricer can also be used to squeeze excess water from sliced or grated potatoes.

Protein: Most North Americans ingest significantly higher amounts than necessary. Studies have linked excess protein with osteoporosis, kidney disease, calcium stones in the urinary tract, and some cancers. A varied diet with adequate calories should provide enough protein, according to the American Dietetic Association. The position of Association, relying on research published in the *American Journal of Clinical Nutrition,* is that complementary proteins do not need to be consumed at the same time and that consumption of various sources of amino acids over the course of the day should ensure adequate nitrogen retention and use in healthy persons. Most foods contain protein. (Fats and sugar do not.) Tempeh, lentils, beans, broccoli and tofu are excellent sources.

Purée: To finely blend food to a smooth, lump-free consistency—usually in a food processor.

Quinoa: A grain high in protein.

Raw foods, nutrition facts: If you use the Internet, The Vegan Society has a page on raw foods. See *www.vegansociety.com.* Information in paper form can be obtained from *Plant Based Nutrition and Health* by Stephen Walsh, published by the Vegan Society, through this link: *http://www.vegansociety.com/shop/product_info. php?cPath=1&products_id=153*

Safflower oil: A flavorless, colorless cooking oil which is high in monounsaturated fat that also has a high smoke point—making it an ideal oil for cooking at higher temperatures.

Scallion: A scallion is one type of immature onion (commonly called green onion), with an edible white base that has not fully developed into a bulb and green leaves that are long and straight. True scallions—generally identified by straight sides of the base, whereas the others have slightly curved bulbs—have a milder taste than other immature onions. Scallions are available year-round but are at their peak during spring and summer. Look for midsized scallions with crisp, bright green tops and long, firm white bases. Scallions, which keep in the refrigerator for up to 5 days, can be cooked whole as a vegetable much as you would a leek. They can also be chopped and used in salads, soups and many other dishes.

Seitan: Known as wheat gluten or wheat meat, seitan is made by rinsing wheat flour dough with water until all the starch dissolves, leaving behind the insoluble gluten. This substance is then boiled or baked in herbs, spices and liquids to impart flavor—making it a versatile addition to many kinds of cuisine. Seitan, which is high in protein, is often used as a replacement for tofu or tempeh. Commercially prepared seitan, such as White Wave, is available in well-stocked supermarkets and major health food stores.

Shiitake mushrooms: See *Vitamin D.*

Soy milk: A plant-based milk, usually appearing in original, vanilla, and chocolate varieties. Easy to find in most large groceries and virtually any health food shop. Slightly heavier than rice milk.

Tamari: Wheat-free soy sauce alternative.

Tempeh: Made from fermented soybeans, and available mixed with spices or vegetables, tempeh has a rough, grainy texture that works well in sandwiches.

Tofu: This versatile staple, made from the curd of the soybean, has no taste until you mix or marinate it with other ingredients, which it absorbs wonderfully. Comes in a range of textures from soft (good for dips) to extra-firm (good for stir-frying).

Tofutti "Better Than Cream Cheese": A cream cheese substitute that is, as we go to press, vegan; and it works in precisely the same way any traditional cream cheese would work.

Tortilla press: A utensil used to press dough into the shape of a tortilla.

Tropical Source: Company using "dedicated" machinery for vegan chocolate (no dairy traces). 10-ounce packages of dark chocolate "semi-sweet chips" sold at grocers with vegetarian products or health food shops. These are small chocolate drops for delicate desserts; they can be found in co-ops and in most groceries with good natural food sections. The company puts effort into informing consumers that chocolate used in their product is purchased only from farms where farmers and workers are treated well.

Vegan (VEE-gun): 1. Pure vegetarian; a recipe using only plant-derived products. 2. A person who has embraced an ethic of concern and respect for sentient life.

Vegan Society: See *www.vegansociety.com.* Basic information about the pure vegetarian diet is available in paper form, including such titles as *Plant Based Nutrition and Health* by Stephen Walsh, published by The Vegan Society, through this link: *http://www.vegansociety.com/shop/product_info.php?cPath=1&products_id=153*

Vegan margarine: There are a few choices of vegan margarines available including Shedds Willow Run, Spectrum Organics Spread, and Earth Balance. When looking for vegan margarine, avoid whey and D-3. Margarines will contain some form of vitamin D fortification; vegans choose D-2 (ergocalciferol). This is important to note, because vitamin D-3, a sheep or fish oil derivative, is less expensive than vitamin D-2, so most margarines will contain D-3. See also *Vitamin D.*

Vegan mayonnaise: Vegan mayonnaise is egg-free and is available in commercially-prepared varieties or can be made at home. Many vegans consider Follow Your Heart's version, Vegenaise®, to be the most flavorful and versatile—making it perfect for most recipes. Vitasoy's Nasoya® line makes a tofu-based mayonnaise that is lower in fat, in addition to selling a fat-free and dijon variety; "Nayonaise" makes an excellent sandwich spread. All vegan mayonnaise is naturally cholesterol-free.

Vegan parmesan: A substitute for grated parmesan cheese, found in many health food shops. Where unavailable, nutritional yeast flakes are sometimes used to provide a similar tangy taste.

Vidalia onion: A versatile, sweet onion grown in a production area defined by law in Georgia.

Vitamin B-12: On rare occasions, vitamin B-12 (needed for cell division and blood formation) does present a concern for pure vegetarians, but the problem is easily solved with a vegan dietary supplement or fortified cereal, or 1 to 2 teaspoons of Red Star T-6635+ nutritional yeast. The body stores this vitamin for a long time, so the use of extra amounts carries over. Breast milk is an adequate source for infants only if the mother's intake is adequate. Absorption of vitamin B-12 becomes less efficient as the body matures, so the American Dietetic Association recommends supplements for all older (albeit young at heart) vegetarians.

Vitamin C: A nutrient that is plentiful in the vegan diet, particularly in citrus fruits and dark green vegetables. See also *iron.*

Vitamin D: According the American Dietetic Association, vitamin D is poorly supplied in all diets unless vitamin D-fortified foods are consumed. Citing the *Journal of Nutrition,* the Association recommends sun exposure to hands, arms, and face for 5 to 15 minutes per day in order to absorb sufficient amounts of the nutrient. People with dark skin or those who live at northern latitudes or in cloudy or smoggy areas may need more exposure. Use of sunscreen interferes with vitamin D synthesis. Thus, if your dermatologist recommends sunscreen, or your sun exposure is inadequate, vitamin D supplements are recommended for vegans, especially our vegan elders. In the winter, the body cannot make vitamin D from sunlight and it may be beneficial for bone health to include about 5 micrograms of the vegan form (ergocalciferol, also known as D-2) daily. This can be obtained from about 10 grams of dried shiitake mushrooms as well as from supplements. Due to the high rate of bone building taking place, infants should receive a vitamin D supplement in winter.

Whey: An animal product (thus not vegan), whey is made of the liquid component of milk.

Kitchen Temperature Conversion Chart

Vegan food can be found anywhere in the world, but depending on the region in which you live, you might use Celsius, Fahrenheit, or gas marks to set your oven. Consult an heirloom cookbook and you're likely to find vague terms (by today's standards—such as slow or moderate. Here is a general guide. It does not comprise exact conversions; also, ovens of different makes and models will vary.

Degrees Fahrenheit	Degrees Celsius	Gas Mark	Description
275	135	1	Slow
300	150	2	Slow
325	160	3	Moderately slow
350	175–180	4	Moderate
375	190	5	Moderately hot
400	205	6	Moderately hot
425	220	7	Hot
450	230	8	Hot
475	245	9	Very hot

English/Metric Conversions

Dry Volume Measurements

⅛ teaspoon=.5 mL
¼ teaspoon= 1 mL
½ teaspoon= 2 mL
¾ teaspoon= 4 mL
1 teaspoon= 5 mL
1 tablespoon= 15 mL
2 tablespoons= 30 mL
¼ cup= 60 mL
⅓ cup= 75 mL
½ cup= 125 mL
¾ cup= 175 mL
1 cup= 250 mL

Fluid Volume Measurements

1 fluid ounce= 30 mL
4 fluid ounces= 125 mL
8 fluid ounces= 250 mL
12 fluid ounces= 375 mL
16 fluid ounces= 500 mL

Weight (Mass) Measurements

½ ounce= 15 g
1 ounce= 30 g
3 ounces= 90 g
4 ounces= 120 g
8 ounces= 225 g
10 ounces= 285 g
12 ounces= 360 g
16 ounces= 450 g
1 pound= 450 g

Friends of Animals 🐾

Contact Information

Friends of Animals
International Headquarters
777 Post Road, Suite 205
Darien, Connecticut U.S. 06820
Phone: 203.656.1522
Fax: 203.656.0267

Internet: www.friendsofanimals.org

E-mail: info@friendsofanimals.org

And please do visit our comprehensive site on what "vegan means"—named, appropriately, *Vegan Means:* www.veganmeans.com

Index